Fortify *your* Faith

Fortify *your* Faith

Building *an* Unshakable Foundation *of*
Radical Grace, Brick *by* Brick

Laurel Appel

Appel Creations
PUBLISHING™

Holly Springs, NC

Published in the United States by Appel Creations LLC, Holly Springs, NC 27540USA

First printing, 2024

Scripture quotations marked NKJV or unmarked are taken from the New King James Version®. Copyright © 1982 by Thomas Nelson. Used by permission. All rights reserved.

Scripture quotations marked NLT are taken from the *Holy Bible*, New Living Translation, Copyright © 1996, 2004, 2015 by Tyndale House Foundation. Used by permission of Tyndale House Publishers, Inc., Carol Stream, Illinois 60188. All rights reserved.

Book Cover Design by ebooklaunch.com
Book Editing by Appel Creations, LLC
Book Interior Formatting by Appel Creations, LLC
Author Photograph by Zach Appel
Graphic Design by Zach Appel
Glyph Butterfly© Illustration by Laurel Appel

ISBN (eBook) 979-8-9855387-4-8

ISBN (PB) 979-8-9855387-3-1

To all those who desperately need God's radical grace.

Met·a·mor·pho·sis

*A change of the form or nature of a thing or person into a completely different one,
by natural or supernatural means.*

Google.com, 2024

Preface

Have you ever found yourself questioning God, Christianity, or your faith? You're not alone. In a 2017 study, the Barna Group discovered that 65% of Christians (or past Christians) had experienced doubts about their faith. Many of us share that journey of having questions about our faith.

"The comforting reality is that questioning what you believe about religion or God is commonplace for most American adults who self-identify as Christian (or have in the past)." (Barna, 2017)

Two-thirds of Americans doubt their faith or relationship with God, which means you most likely have doubted, too. There is no shame in questioning the most important decisions of our human lives. However, wouldn't it be fabulous to settle into a steadfast and unwavering faith once and for all? Is that even possible?

Here's some incredible news for you. It's not just a possibility, but once you grasp God's amazing, revolutionary, and radical grace, you'll discover a stable faith that can withstand any challenge life throws at you, or false doctrine that tries to steal away your security in Jesus.

So, how does learning about grace fortify your faith? The more you understand and solidify your understanding of God's grace, the more you will receive it and take it to heart. The more you sink the truths of how His grace blesses you, the more your faith is bolstered because you know and believe that God loves you not based on what you do but simply because you are His creation. You can trust Him even when things in your life are difficult or you are struggling, because you know He loves you more than you can fathom, and you are His child.

Why do I call God's grace radical? The word *radical* means that it *relates to the root or source of something*. God's radical grace is the foundation of our entire relationship with Him. His grace brings us into His family, and by that same grace, we get to live out the rest of our lives basking in the glorious benefits that Jesus has provided us.

In slang, *radical* refers to something *cool* or *excellent*. God's grace *is* excellent. Let's celebrate the tremendous gift that it is by fully receiving it and walking in it forevermore.

This study guide is the culmination of years of study and research and inspired by the preparation for my book *Radical Grace: Live Free and Unashamed*. This study includes the scriptural doctrine that underpins that book. A deeper understanding of the Gospel and what Jesus did for me has transformed and strengthened my faith, and now I'm thrilled to share this transformative experience with you.

I will take you through the same tour of the Bible that created an unwavering faith in my own life. This study examines the Biblical building blocks that form the foundation of God's radical grace. Comprehending what Jesus has done for you completely changes everything. God's radical grace will rock your world, fortify your faith, and draw you closer than ever to your Lord and Savior, Jesus.

May God bless you as you walk in His radical grace!

Laurel

How to Use This Book

As I sat down to put this study together, I was trying to envision you, the reader, and how you might like to go about a Bible study. Sounds like a good idea, right? But you are unique and beautiful and do things differently than others. For example, you might be working through this study alone, with a study buddy, or participating within a group. Additionally, you might be a note taker or like to read through and contemplate in your brain without writing stuff down. All are viable ways to learn. This study is flexible so that you can do it your way.

Brick by Brick

In *Matthew 7:24*, Jesus likened those who hear Him and do what He asks to someone who has built their home on a rock instead of being built on shifting sand. I have found that having a solid understanding of, and belief in, some foundational concepts has allowed me to live confidently with faith in and relationship with Jesus; no doubts, no wavering faith, only trust and loyal worship of a God, who I know loves me. That is what I desire for you.

Picture a brick foundation. Each chapter will examine and discuss three "bricks" that are fundamental to the foundation of God's Radical Grace. You will be constructing a foundation upon which you are built up as a spiritual house, like in *1 Peter 2:5*. The brick topics we will study are as follows:

Part 1: Brick by Brick

Jesus

Righteousness

Promise

Old Covenant

New Covenant

New You

Spirit

Love

The first eight chapters each contain three specific bricks that will help you to build up your foundational understanding of grace. It is essential to set and cement each brick in place. You will place each following brick upon the previous ones. This process will ensure that by the end of this study, you will have a solid foundation of radical grace, and your faith will be immovable.

The last four chapters contain helpful tools and exercises for you to reinforce what you learned in the first eight chapters. They are meant to encourage you in your new walk in Christ. They are titled:

Part 2: Unshakable Foundation

Freedom

The Gospel of Radical Grace

Keys

Radical Grace & Fortified Faith

The key to not getting "*tossed to and fro and carried about with every wind of doctrine*" (**Eph 4:14** NKJV) is to fully understand and cement your belief in the subjects presented in this study. A firm foundation in God's grace will help you avoid slipping into a legalistic approach to your faith. Not only that, but it will help you to walk in the freedom, peace, and unbridled joy that Jesus died and rose again to provide for you.

Fortify Your Faith provides a versatile format, allowing you to customize your study based on your schedule. The curriculum consists of 30 lessons divided into 12 chapters, offering the flexibility to complete the study in various timeframes. Whether you prefer a more accelerated pace by completing one lesson daily for 1 month, a moderate rate of one chapter weekly for a 12-week study, or a slower progression of one lesson per week over 30 weeks, the study caters to your preferred learning rhythm.

Tools and Tips

Consider the following to get the most from your time in this study:

> 1. Start with prayer. Ask the Holy Spirit to guide you through this study and to help you understand and

receive the truth of the Word.

2. Using the New King James Version (NKJV) of the Bible or an online Bible app that includes that version would be beneficial. I wrote the questions using the NKJV translation.

3. If you are a note taker, you should have what you need to take notes. Also, keep highlighters handy if you like to highlight in your Bible. If you want to look up words and other information that enrich your experience, you may wish to have a Bible dictionary, concordance, and other resources available.

4. To keep the page count, and therefore the cost, of this book down for you, I do not typically type out the scriptures; I only provide the references. These references will be ***bolded and italicized***. You will get the most out of this study if you take the time to look up every passage and verse, read through it, and spend some time thinking about what it says in conjunction with what the study is guiding you to consider.

5. The first eight chapters have one main topic that you will study in three lessons (bricks). There are 24 bricks that you will study and place into your foundation of radical grace. The final four chapters, formatted differently, offer helpful tools and exercises. Some chapters (topics) will require more study than others. Take the time needed to explore each chapter fully, and don't feel like you must move through in a hurry. As you grasp the facts of each brick, I will ask you to figuratively cement them down so that you will never let anything lead you astray from the truth of the Gospel, which, in turn, will fortify your faith.

6. Allow yourself to approach this study with an open mind. This study challenges conventional thinking in some ways, so you will want to approach the information thoughtfully as you dig deep and discover the astonishing truth about God's grace. In this study, we follow the truth, even if it goes against long-held beliefs. I always give biblical backing to those challenges so you may see what the Scriptures say about them and decide for yourself about each concept. Be like the people of Berea in ***Acts 17:11***. They were ready to receive what Paul had to say to them, but they searched the Scriptures to see if what he said was true. I encourage you to be like a Berean.

7. In each lesson, I ask you to place a check mark to confirm that you believe the Scriptures support each lesson topic and the foundational truth I submit. You must consciously decide to receive each truth as you go through this study. This exercise will ensure that each brick you place in your foundational understanding of grace will be unmovable; therefore, your faith in and relationship with Jesus will be ironclad. In turn, you won't be susceptible to being led astray with false doctrine or legalistic teachings that directly oppose Jesus' mission to free you in His grace.

8. Finally, if you haven't read my book, *Radical Grace: Live Free and Unashamed*, you might want to do so in tandem with doing this study. Although you can do this study to learn about God's grace without reading *Radical Grace*, that book provides additional information and discussion of relational topics that benefit

your complete understanding of radical grace. Each chapter of this study will give you the correlating chapters to read in *Radical Grace* before or while tackling the material presented. You may purchase a paperback, hardcover, or eBook version of *Radical Grace: Live Free and Unashamed* anywhere books are sold.

Small Group Discussion Guide

I offer a free downloadable small group discussion guide .PDF on my website, which is to be used after the completion of each chapter. Whether you are completing this study with a partner or in a group, these questions encourage you to engage with the material and reflect on what you have read. Visit LaurelAppel.com to download your copy today.

Let's Dive In!

Through this study, you will cultivate and create a solid relationship with God, your Savior, Jesus, and the Holy Spirit. It's time to grab your Bible and pen or pencil and start building that foundation of radical grace and fortifying your faith.

Contents

Part 1

Brick by Brick

"For no other foundation can anyone lay than that which is laid, which is Jesus Christ."

1 Corinthians 3:11

Chapter 1

Jesus

"God, who at various times and in various ways spoke in time past to the fathers by the prophets, has in these last days spoken to us by His Son, whom He has appointed heir of all things, through whom also He made the worlds"

Hebrews 1:1-4

When Jesus came, died, and rose again, everything changed. How we approach God and our relationship with Him is much different than before Jesus' death and resurrection. Everything we know and experience is affected by Jesus, from the Creation itself to our relationship with Him and others. He brought the magnificence of God down into our existence, turned the world upside down while He was here, and after leaving, He sent His Spirit to dwell in the hearts and lives of those whom He calls His friends and brethren.

We can summarize the Gospel of Grace in one word: Jesus. However, the magnitude of who Jesus is and what He has done for us will never be fully understood or explained. We can't fathom all that He is, but we will learn more about Him through this study, and as we do, we will grow to love and appreciate His grace more than ever.

In this chapter, I demonstrate that Jesus is the subject of, reason for, and foundation of radical grace.

Read chapters 1-3 of *Radical Grace* if you are reading it together with this study.

Pre-study Thoughts

How would you describe the Gospel of Grace to someone who asked you about Jesus?

Jesus is the Cornerstone
Brick 1

"This is the 'stone which is rejected by you builders, which has become the chief cornerstone."

Acts 4:11

The cornerstone is the first brick placed when laying a foundation for a building or a house. It determines the direction, elevation, and placement of the entire structure. When placed, each following brick is secured with mortar and set in line with the cornerstone.

The Foundational Truth

Jesus is the cornerstone of the Gospel of Grace.

If you declare you are a follower of Jesus, you most likely know that the Christian faith is about Jesus, His sacrificial death on the cross, and His resurrection. You also know and believe that He redeems those who call Him Lord. We will begin this study by examining why Jesus is the basis for our faith as we learn that Jesus is the cornerstone of the foundation of the Gospel of Radical Grace.

The Old Testament contains prophecies about one called the cornerstone, and the New Testament confirms who that cornerstone is through several New Testament writers. Let's examine the Word of God and see for ourselves if Jesus is the cornerstone.

The Cornerstone

Everything about our faith, God's Word, and His grace is about Jesus. That is why Jesus is called the cornerstone of the good news message of the Gospel of Grace.

We begin this lesson reading Old Testament prophecies concerning the cornerstone.

> Read **Psalm 118:22** and **Isaiah 28:16**. I love how the Isaiah scripture mentions that the stone is a tried and precious stone. What are your thoughts about the stone being *tried* and *precious* in relation to Jesus?

Now, let's look at the fulfillment of those prophetic statements in the New Testament. Three different men indicated that Jesus is the rejected stone who became the chief cornerstone.

Jesus

> Read **Matthew 21:42-46**. (Also found in **Mark 12:10-12** and **Luke 20:17-19**.)

In these passages, Jesus doesn't expressly claim that He is the chief cornerstone, but I believe He indeed indicates that fact. The chief priests and Pharisees knew Jesus was speaking about their rejection of the Messiah, to which they took offense.

> Do you suppose they might have thought about this conversation later and recognized that Jesus was claiming to be their Messiah?   Yes   No

Peter

> Read **Acts 4:8-12**. What does Peter confirm about Jesus?

> Next read **1 Peter 2:4-10**. According to verse 7, what does Peter say Jesus became to those who believe?

According to verse 8, what two things does Jesus become to those who don't believe in Him?

What do you think causes people to stumble and be offended with Jesus?

Who are the two groups mentioned in verse 7?

Stumbling is equated with disbelief. The NKJV translation uses the word *disobedience*, but we should note that it is not disobedience to the Law or works; it is disobedience to faith or disbelief. The Greek word for *disobedient* in this passage means *to refuse to be persuaded*, *to refuse belief*, or t*o be disobedient*. (Vine, Unger, & White, Jr., 1984, 1996, p. 173)

Faith in Christ both offended and caused the Jewish leaders to stumble because they were steeped in the idea that they could obtain righteousness by obeying the Law. They stumbled with the idea that simply having faith in Jesus is the way to righteousness and were offended because their power over the people was in jeopardy if people followed Jesus by faith instead of them through works of the Law. Therefore, Jesus is the *"stone of stumbling"* and *"rock of offense."*

In *1 Peter 2:9*, Peter tells us those who receive Jesus are called what four things?

Do you identify with these four descriptions of you as a follower of Christ?   Yes   No
If not, why do you think that is?

At the end of verse 9, Peter explains what we may do now that we are a chosen, royal, holy, and special people. What is that?

According to verse 10, those who receive Jesus are now a people of God and have obtained what?

I get excited when I read passages like this section in Peter. We need to be reminded of our new titles more often.

Paul

Next read *Romans 9:30-33*. As we have already read, Peter pointed out that Jesus became a stumbling stone. Here, Paul explains this further. How have the Gentiles, or non-Jewish people, attained righteousness according to verse 30?

Why did Israel not achieve righteousness?

Consider this passage and the importance of faith in obtaining righteousness. We will visit this topic more throughout this study as we explore the value and significance of our faith.

Next read *1 Corinthians 3:11*. Paul describes Jesus as what?

Read *Ephesians 2:19-22*. Those who receive Jesus are a dwelling place of Whom?

According to Peter and Paul, Jesus is the stone the builders rejected and has become the chief cornerstone. The Jewish nation, for the most part, rejected their Messiah. Hence, Jesus is the stone they rejected and crucified.

Through His death and resurrection, He became the chief cornerstone of the Gospel of Radical Grace. It should come as no surprise, then, that Jesus is called the chief cornerstone in Scripture.

Through receiving Jesus by faith, we obtain His mercy and His righteousness. Jesus is not just a cornerstone, but the very foundation upon which we are built up as the temple of God. Everything about our faith and relationship with God is because of Jesus and what He has done for us. Therefore, Jesus and His radical grace should always be the foundational basis for what we do, in what we read and hear, and how we perceive the world around us.

Why Does it Matter to You?

Why do you think it is important that you know that Jesus is the cornerstone of the Gospel of Radical Grace?

Why it Matters to Grace

Jesus and grace are eternally entangled. Without Jesus, we couldn't receive God's grace, and without God's grace, we wouldn't have the opportunity to receive Jesus. The Gospel is the good news of the grace of God through His Son, Jesus, which we obtain by faith in His righteousness, and He bestows upon us when we believe. We build our relationship with God upon Jesus, the cornerstone of the Gospel and provider of radical grace.

Confirm the Brick

You have examined many scriptures that speak about the cornerstone. Do you believe that Jesus is the chief cornerstone? If so, put a check mark next to the following statement to confirm this belief as part of your understanding of the foundation of radical grace.

Yes, Jesus is the chief cornerstone.

Jesus is God and Man
Brick 2

*"Let this mind be in you which was also in Christ Jesus, who, being in the form of God,
did not consider it robbery to be equal with God, but made Himself of no reputation,
taking the form of a bondservant, and coming in the likeness of men."*

Philippians 2:5-7

God's grace astounds me. God, the Creator of the universe, loves me, you, and our fellow humans so much that He came down from His holy habitation, humbled Himself as a human being, and offered Himself as a sacrifice to usher in the New Covenant and all its blessings. Wow! That is astonishing love and an incredible act of radical grace.

The Foundational Truth

Jesus is God who came to earth as a man.

For Jesus to do this spectacular act of love, He had to be God and man. In this lesson, we will examine the fact that He is both. We must believe that He is both to satisfy the requirements of our salvation. We can see these truths in events such as His birth, ministry, death, and resurrection. Let's dig in to see Jesus as the Son of God and the Son of Man.

Jesus as God

We begin our study in the book of John.

Read *John 1:1-2*. These two verses say that the Word was not only with God, but was who?

Read *John 1:3*. Summarize this verse.

Look at *Genesis 1* verses *1*, *3*, *9*, *11*, *14*, *20*, *24* and *26*. What are the first three words?

God spoke creation into existence. His Words created the heavens and the earth. We have established that the Word is God, and all things were made through Him, but we haven't defined who, specifically, John is talking about in these verses.

Next read *John 1:10*. What does this verse tell us about this person called the Word?

Read *John 1:14*. This verse tells us the Word became flesh and lived among the people of the world. Who must John be talking about?

Don't miss the last five words of the verse. Why do you think John mentions grace and truth here?

Note the significance of *1 John 5:7*. Which three are one?

We know the Word is God, who created the heavens and the earth, and the Word became flesh and lived among the people. The Word is Jesus, the Christ, or Messiah.

Read *Colossians 2:9* and *Colossians 1:19*. What dwells in Jesus bodily?

Read *Acts 19:4*. Who does Paul say Christ is?

Do you think Jesus ever claimed to be God?   Yes   No

Look at *John 5:5-18*, and *10:30-33*. What, or who, did Jesus claim to be?

Read *Mark 2:5-12*. How does this passage speak to the fact that Jesus is God?

The Pharisees recognized that only God could forgive sins. If Jesus forgave sins, that meant He claimed to be God.

Next look at *John 8:53-59*, noting verse *58*. What did Jesus call Himself?

Now read *Exodus 3:13-14*. What is the significance and relevance of this passage to the previous question?

Note that at the risk of the penalty of death, Jesus claimed to be God's Son, placing Himself equal with God the Father. In other words, He claimed to be God. For this reason, He was condemned to death on the cross. The very act of declaring He was God was what facilitated God's plan for the New Covenant.

We can be confident that Jesus is God.

Before we move on, I'd like to highlight one more passage that will assist our understanding of Jesus as God and man. It bridges the gap, so to speak.

Read *Luke 1:34-35*. According to these two verses, who are the parents of Jesus?

I'm not going to waste your time going into a detailed science discussion, so I'll make this extremely simplified point: It takes a mom and a dad to create a baby human. Jesus' mother is Mary, who is human, and His father is God, by way of the Holy Spirit. According to this passage in Luke, Jesus is both God and human.

Why did Jesus have to be God to save us? Jesus had to be perfectly righteous to pay the penalty for our sins (*redemption*) and to take on God's wrath for our sins (*propitiation*). God is the only one who is perfectly righteous and could have done these things.

We see then that Jesus is God, but why did God have to become a human to save us? Let's find out.

Jesus as Man

Jesus had to be a human to offer Himself as the sacrificial Lamb to redeem humankind. Why is this true?

Read *Leviticus 17:11*. The life of the flesh is in what?

What is it that makes atonement for the soul?

Read *1 Timothy 1:17*. According to this verse, can God die?   Yes   No

Read *1 Peter 3:18*. How did Jesus bring us to God?

Read *Hebrews 9:22*. Without the shedding of blood, there is no what?

Read *Matthew 26:28*. Jesus said His blood was shed for what purpose?

Read *Romans 3:21-24*. According to verse 24, through the redemption in Christ, we are what?

Jesus had to be human to offer His blood. He had to be able to bleed and die. Therefore, He was born as a human baby. (See *Matthew 1:18-25*)

Because the blood of sacrificial animals can't take away sins (*Hebrews 10:4*), there had to be a better and perfect sacrifice. The animal sacrifices could only purify the flesh, which was only for a time, so the priests had to return year after year to continually make those sacrifices. *Hebrews 9:11-15* explains that Jesus only had to offer His blood once to obtain redemption forever for those called His. In addition, His blood sacrifice cleanses our conscience from dead works, sin, and useless acts.

The writer goes on to say that this is why the Mediator of the New Covenant is Jesus and that He had to die to redeem the sins committed under the Old Covenant Law and to offer the inheritance of eternal life. **Hebrews 10:5** says that God the Father prepared a body for Him so that He could put an end to the continual sin-sacrifice cycle of the Old Covenant Law. He took away the Old Covenant to establish the New Covenant (**Hebrews 10:9**).

Paul also covers this concept in his letter to the Romans. In **Romans 8:3** Paul tells us that Jesus had to come in the likeness of sinful flesh so He could condemn sin in the flesh.

Read **Hebrews 2:9**. What does the writer of Hebrews say is the reason Jesus came as a man?

What does the writer mean by saying that Jesus was made a little lower than the angels?

Read **Philippians 2:5-8**. Does this passage say that Jesus is God?   Yes   No

Does it say He came as a man?   Yes   No

Jesus experienced very human struggles including birth and death, pain, temptation, hunger, and thirst. See **Matthew 1:24-25**, **4:1**, **16:21**, **21:18**, **27:50**, and **John 19:28**. Jesus had a physical body that bled. Read **John 19:34**, **Ephesians 2:13**, and **Hebrews 13:12**.

There is no doubt that Jesus was human.

Why did Jesus have to be human to save us? Jesus had to be human so He could shed His blood and die. Only a righteous sacrifice would suffice to pay the cost of the redemption of humanity. No man or woman on earth could have paid the penalty that Jesus paid. We praise and thank Jesus that He was qualified and willing.

Jesus was born of Mary and the Holy Spirit and was considered both the Son of Man (**Matthew 9:6**) and the Son of God (**Luke 1:35**, & **22:70**). Jesus is righteous (**1 John 2:1**). Only a righteous God could justify the ungodly (**Romans 4:5**).

Why Does it Matter to You?

Why is it important that you grasp that Jesus is God who came as a man?

Why it Matters to Grace

The beauty of understanding that Jesus is completely God and completely man is that we know that our Creator, God, loves us so much that he humbled Himself to come to earth as a human so He could redeem us through His death and justify us through His resurrection. Understanding how Jesus could be all man and all God is impossible for us to grasp but believing it to be true is vital to understanding His grace. What Jesus did for the world, for you and me, is a beautiful act of grace, and He had to be both man and God to fulfill His mission of offering salvation through the redemption of the world. That is revolutionary. That is radical grace.

Confirm the Brick

Do you believe that Jesus had to be both God and man to fulfill His mission? If so, put a check mark next to the statement below.

Yes, Jesus is God who came as a man.

"It's all about Jesus"
Brick 3

"For the word of God is living and powerful, and sharper than any two-edged sword, piercing even to the division of soul and spirit, and of joints and marrow, and is a discerner of the thoughts and intents of the heart."

Hebrews 4:12

In my book Radical Grace, I mention that *"It's all about Jesus, Genesis to Revelation"* (Appel, 2022, pg. 22) when speaking of the Bible. I talk about the fact that you can find Jesus, or the need for Him, throughout the Scriptures.

While walking on the road to Emmaus, Jesus took Cleopas and his friend on a guided tour through the Old Testament Scriptures, from Moses through the prophets, to show them a clear picture of Himself, their Messiah (See **Luke 24:13-27**) and why He needed to die on the cross.

The book of Hebrews also speaks about the Bible being about Jesus (See **Hebrews 10:5-7**). However, Jesus is not only found throughout the Word, but He is also called the Word.

The Foundational Truth

The Word of God is all about Jesus.

Recall in lesson two, *Jesus is God and Man*, we examined the scriptures that speak about Jesus being the Word of God to establish that He is God, but we didn't explore the profound meaning of the fact that He is the Word. In this lesson, we will explore the idea that the Bible is all about Jesus. We will see that both the New and Old Testaments are about Him and His mission as our Savior. We will discover that Jesus, and the need for His redemption, is found throughout the entire Bible. Realizing these truths can provide a different perspective on the Bible and help us receive what the Word says.

Let's explore Jesus **in** the Word as well as Jesus **as** the Word.

Jesus *in* the Word

Studying Jesus in the Old Testament could be a book all on its own, but that isn't the purpose of this study. However, I thought it would be interesting to see a sampling of the scriptures about our Lord, Jesus, in the Old Testament. The following is a mini tour of a few prophecies and verses that show their fulfillment. I encourage you to dig deeper into the Word and discover all of them for yourself.

The first reference to Jesus is in *Genesis 3:15*. He is the Seed of Eve, or the descendant of Eve, that is at enmity with Satan and his seed. Also read *Isaiah 7:14*, *Luke 1:31-35*, and *Galatians 4:4-5*.

Read *Genesis 49:8* and *Micah 5:2*. From what tribe of Israel will the Messiah be according to the Old Testament?

Now read *Matthew 1:1-2*, *Luke 3:23 & 33-34*, *Hebrews 7:14*, and *Revelation 5:5*. From what tribe is Jesus?

In the Micah scripture you read, it mentions a town from where the ruler of Israel would go forth. What town is mentioned?

Now read *Matthew 2:1*. Where was Jesus born?

Hosea 11:1 gives us an interesting prophecy. The LORD God is speaking about the nation of Israel, but then He says that He will call His son out of Egypt. Now look up *Matthew 2:14-15*. Where does this verse say Jesus lived with His parents for a time?

Read *Psalm 69:4* and *John 15:24-25*. Even the fact that Jesus would be hated was foretold!

I will leave you with one more stunning passage that I'm sure Jesus mentioned to the men as He walked with them on the way to Emmaus.

> Read *Psalm 22*. Can you find New Testament verses that show the correlation between what David foretold and what Jesus experienced while on the cross? List them here.

These and many more prophesies about Jesus tremendously impacted me as a new believer in Christ. I was amazed at how people thousands of years ago could write down, often in a poetic form, things that happened concerning Jesus. Seeing these prophecies revealed to me the incredible power of God and that He knows the beginning from the end (See *Isaiah 46:10*).

Jesus *as* the Word

I did not know Christ as a child. My mother was a believer, but she didn't talk about Jesus or the Bible much, and we didn't go to church, even for Easter or Christmas. If she read her Bible, I didn't know. I'm sure she did, but her seemingly nonchalant attitude about it didn't elevate the Bible, or Jesus, for that matter, to any level of importance in my mind.

With that background, as a believer, I decided I wanted to know more; I wanted to learn about Jesus and find out what I could about this person that I placed my trust in concerning my daily life and eternal destiny. So, I went spelunking into the Word of God. Come along with me now as I show you this fascinating God-man Jesus called the Word.

Recall in *John 1:1* and *1:14* that Jesus is called the Word. He spoke Creation into existence, but He also is the Word who speaks to us personally about what is important in this life.

> Read *Hebrews 1:1-2*. In the past, how did God speak to people?

And now that Jesus has come, how does God speak to people?

Jesus' life, ministry, death, and resurrection speak beautiful things to us. Jesus is so much more than a story of a person that we can read about in a dusty old book sitting on grandma's coffee table. Jesus is the Word, and when we read our Bible, we engage ourselves with Jesus.

Read *Hebrews 4:12*. This verse lists five things that the Word of God is. What are those five things?

The beginning of Hebrews 4:12 says that the Word of God is living and powerful. How can this be true? We have established that Jesus is the Word of God through John 1:1 & 14. He is both living and powerful. This verse means the Bible is living. It is alive because it is Jesus; it is God, Himself, and the Spirit of God. I remind you that *1 John 5:7* states that God, the Word, and the Spirit are one.

The Word is also powerful in our lives because Jesus has power. Read *Acts 10:34-38*.

The Word is sharp. It is sharper than any other sword and it can divide what we humanly cannot. It can distinguish between soul and spirit, or bone and marrow. How can this be? Read *Ephesians 6:17* and *Revelation 2:12-16*, specifically note verses 12 and 16.

Now consider that Hebrews 4:12 says that the Word of God is a discerner of our thoughts and can perceive our hearts' intentions. When we read the Word of God, it is reading us! This is a beautiful picture of relationship and intimacy with God.

When we spend time in the Word, we spend time with our Lord. He speaks to us through the Bible, guides us, and comforts us. His Word teaches us and reveals His overwhelming love for us. God knows our hearts and thoughts, and He, through the Spirit, directs us and reveals Himself to us.

I used to see the Bible as a mysterious, hard-to-read old book. But now I am drawn into it because it intrigues me to discover more and more about Jesus. I realize that there is no way I will ever exhaust my learning about and exploring the Word, but I enjoy spending time with my Savior and listening to His voice every time I immerse myself in the Word of God, and you can too.

Why Does it Matter to You?

Why is it important that you recognize that the entire Bible is about Jesus, and that the Word *is* Jesus?

Why it Matters to Grace

That Jesus is both in the Word and is the Word supports and strengthens the idea that Jesus's death and resurrection were God's plan since at least the fall of man, if not before. The promise of the New Covenant was in place at the beginning of creation. Since we see Jesus prophesied about and mentioned throughout the Old Testament, we know that His act of sacrifice was already in His and God the Father's minds well before He was crucified. Additionally, we can see that God is consistent. He has never wavered from the initial plan.

We see that Jesus, because He is God, is the one who made the promise, He is the one who was willing to die to bring us into His family, and He is the one who gives us many blessings for being a part of it. That is radical grace.

Confirm the Brick

What do you think about our premise that *"It's all about Jesus"*? Do you believe that the Word of God is all about Jesus and that Jesus is the Word? If so, place a check mark next to the foundational statement below and firmly place that truth into your knowledge of radical grace.

Yes, the Bible is all about Jesus, and Jesus is the Word.

Build the Foundation of Radical Grace

It is time to cement these bricks about Jesus into your understanding of radical grace. Laying these Jesus bricks down as the first few bricks is most likely a no-brainer for you, as you understand that Jesus is the reason for and definition of your faith.

I labeled these first three bricks *Jesus* because without Him, there would be no Gospel of Radical Grace.

19

Bricks 1, 2, and 3: *Jesus*

The facts:

Jesus is the cornerstone of the Gospel of Grace.

Jesus is both God and man.

Jesus is in the Word and He is the Word. The Bible is all about Jesus.

Remember, once in place, you can't move these bricks. Any teaching, writing, song lyric, or social media post that opposes these bricks of truth cannot be accurate and means to draw you away from the truth of the Gospel and Jesus' radical grace.

Live Free and Unashamed

Jesus experienced being human. Sometimes, He was too hot or cold, suffered pain, felt angry, and was disappointed in others. He lost people He loved, endured humiliation, and experienced the betrayal of a close friend. Jesus can relate to what you are going through right now. The Scriptures tells us that He experienced being human. He aids those who are tested, is merciful, sympathizes with our weaknesses, and has compassion because He was subject to the same weaknesses. Remember these things this week as you pray about life's hardships and struggles. Remember, He empathizes with you. Be comforted by this fact.

Jesus, like us, also experienced moments of joy, laughter, and contentment. These are the good things in life, and I believe they are gifts from God. Have you ever imagined Jesus laughing or smiling? What does that image mean to you? This week, I encourage you to also realize that He is present in your moments of joy, smiling alongside you. This can be a powerful way to feel His presence and find comfort in His understanding of your experiences.

Chapter 2

Righteousness

"But now the righteousness of God apart from the law is revealed, being witnessed by the Law and the Prophets, even the righteousness of God, through faith in Jesus Christ, to all and on all who believe."

Romans 3:21-22

I spent the first twenty years of my life striving to gain righteousness through what I did and didn't do. Inside, I felt so unworthy of God's love and sacrifice that I immersed myself in trying to look good on the outside to hide my inner secret unrighteousness that dominated my mind and actions. After all, that is what we Christians do, right? Though we are saved and will go to heaven, in the meantime, certain teachers tell us that because Jesus has done so much for us, it is our job to behave well to show or prove our salvation and, more importantly, that we are thankful to Him. The Christian community tells us that we accomplish this by being obedient and trying to live up to a high moral standard.

God's radical grace means you can stop trying to make your flesh better. In today's study, we will start to unwind faulty teaching and begin to build our foundation of His radical grace with a correct understanding of righteousness. To understand God's grace, we must fully grasp the next bricks about *Righteousness*. God is perfectly righteous and requires that standard from us to be with Him in eternity. These bricks are critical because without understanding God's requirement of righteousness and our state of unrighteousness without Jesus, we would not choose to put our faith in Him. We wouldn't think we need a Savior. Like the Pharisees who rejected Jesus because they believed they were already righteous through the Law, Jesus is a stumbling stone for those who think they can be righteous on their own. And this is precisely the point where many Christians stumble.

This chapter will explore righteousness from the perspective of God's perfection and our imperfection. This understanding will make clear the reason we need Jesus.

Read chapter 4 of *Radical Grace* if you are reading it with this study.

God's Righteousness
Brick 4

"Therefore you shall be perfect, just as your Father in heaven is perfect."

Matthew 5:48

We must understand that our faith is not simply believing Jesus exists but also that He is righteous. If He wasn't righteous, He could not have atoned for our sins nor become the cornerstone of the Gospel. Additionally, to be with Him, we must also be righteous. God holds us to a very high standard of righteousness.

The Foundational Truth

God is perfectly righteous, and He requires the same of us to be with Him in eternity.

Everything God does or says is the standard of perfect righteousness. Jesus had to be righteous to offer Himself as the perfect atoning sacrifice for all of humanity. In addition to this fact, His standard of righteousness for us to be with Him is for us to be perfectly righteous as well. In today's lesson, we will explore these concepts about God's righteousness and His standard of righteousness for salvation.

The way to reach that standard of righteousness is the topic of many sermons, songs, and studies. We will address the "how" in lesson three of this chapter. Today's lesson will focus on the "what" and "why" of righteousness. In this first lesson, we will explore this critical part of the foundation of radical grace.

The Righteousness of God

God is the definition of righteousness. He is right, true, holy, innocent, and without fault. This profound truth, which you may already be aware of, is worth discussing because taking the time to think about God's righteousness will help us to understand the big picture of His radical grace.

Numerous scriptures tell us that the LORD God is righteous. Let's look at a handful of them.

Read **Deuteronomy 32:3-4**. How is the LORD God described?

Read **2 Chronicles 12:6**, **Psalm 11:7**, and **Lamentations 1:18**.

Next read **Ezra 9:15**, **Nehemiah 9:8**, **Psalm 119:137**, **Jeremiah 12:1**. What common word do these writers call the LORD?

Read **Psalm 116:5**. What three characteristics does this verse ascribe to the LORD God?

Read **Psalm 71:19**. How does the psalmist describe God's righteousness?

Read **Romans 1:16-17**. What is revealed in the Gospel?

Read **2 Peter 1:1**. Does Peter say that Jesus is righteous?   Yes   No

Read **John 17:25**. How does Jesus address His Father?

God is not only righteous, but everything He does is righteous.

Read **Jeremiah 23:5**. This is a prophecy about Jesus. He is called *a Branch of righteousness*. What two things will He execute in the earth?

Read **Daniel 9:14**. As Daniel was praying, asking God for forgiveness for Israel for not obeying His Law, he admitted that everything the LORD God does is what?

Read *Psalm 145:17*. In what ways is the LORD God righteous?

Read *Zephaniah 3:5*. God will do no what?

God is the definition of righteousness. He is perfectly righteous, and everything He does is righteous as well. He is the standard of righteousness. Next, we will look at what His standard of righteousness is for us.

God's Standard

Most followers of Jesus agree that He is perfectly righteous and took our sins to the cross to pay the required price. That is what reconciliation means. However, we need more than our sins paid for to enter God's presence. Jesus *declares us innocent* because He paid our debt, bringing us up to ground zero in a legal sense. Although He wipes our record clean of our sinful actions, we are still unrighteous. We need one more step to inherit eternal life and be in the presence of our Holy God. That step is to *be righteous*, and God's standard of righteousness is very high.

Look at the following verses that state this fact.

Read *1 Corinthians 6:9-10*. Who, does this verse say, cannot inherit the kingdom of God?

This verse means that only the righteous may inherit the kingdom of God. But how righteous must we be? Let's find out.

Read *Matthew 5:20*. How righteous must we be to enter the kingdom of heaven?

Do you get the feeling that the standard of righteousness is very high to hang out with God? It is indeed very high.

Next read *Matthew 5:48*. How perfect must we be?

That bar of perfection is extremely high, wouldn't you say? Our righteousness must match that of God for us to enter eternity with Him. Can we match it?

Read *Job 4:17*. Job is asked if mortals can be more righteous or pure than God. How would you answer these questions?

Perfect righteousness on our own is impossible, right? That's the point.

Jesus tells it like it is. He graciously explains His lofty standard of righteousness because He wants to save us. Jesus knows our righteousness in the flesh will never be good enough to be in good standing with God or obtain salvation. Therefore, He directs us away from the impossible undertaking of trying to gain perfect righteousness on our own and directs us toward Him. He shows us the impossible standard, then offers us the only way to meet that standard: by putting our faith in His righteousness for our own. When we do, He pays the price for our sins and places His righteousness on our account. He makes us righteous when He makes us new.

Read *Matthew 25:46*. Who receives eternal life?

Why Does it Matter to You?

Why, do you suppose, it is important for you to know that God's standard is perfect righteousness? Does this fact change your understanding of the Gospel?

Why it Matters to Grace

It makes sense that we must be perfectly righteous to be with a perfectly righteous God. This fact is the first link in the chain that shows us His great and radical grace.

First, He requires perfect righteousness. We need Him to obtain it so, Jesus came to make it possible for Him to give us that perfect righteousness. We receive it by putting our faith in Jesus because of these truths.

God's love, which is the driving force behind His actions, led Him to elevate us to His standard through the sacrifice of His Son. This act of love, this radical grace, is the very definition of His character.

Confirm the Brick

Put a check mark by the following statement and add this brick into your understanding of the foundation of radical grace if you believe it is true.

God is perfectly righteous, and He requires the same of us to be with Him in eternity.

Our Unrighteousness
Brick 5

"...for all have sinned and fall short of the glory of God..."

Romans 3:23

When we were very young children, we had no idea when or if we were in a dangerous situation. Our parents might have saved us from serious injury by snatching us away from an oncoming car or forbidding us from doing something that they knew would hurt us. We don't appreciate the people who cared for us when we were young until we are older and wiser. We understand how vulnerable we were as kids and the possibility of serious things happening. As adults, we know and appreciate the predicaments we may have been in and the benefit and blessing of those who kept us safe.

Likewise, I state in my book, *Radical Grace, "To appreciate the magnitude and beauty of what Jesus did for the world, we need to grasp the predicament we were in without Him."* (Appel, 2022, p. 29) We need to know we need a Savior.

The Foundational Truth

We are all born unrighteous.

One of the consequences of Adam's disobedience is that all of humanity is now born into a world where sin exists. No human can claim they are born righteous. This is the predicament that Jesus, in his divine mission, came to resolve.

In this lesson, we look at our inability to meet God's standard of righteousness through our efforts. We examine our "old man or woman" and see just how unrighteous our flesh is.

The Fall of Man

Many Christians call Adam and Eve's disobedience in the Garden of Eden the *Fall of Man*. It is vital that we understand that we are not perfectly righteous; we can't measure up to God's required standard on our own. We will start by looking at our situation before we come to faith in Jesus.

Read **Romans 5:12**.

Who is the "one man" Paul is talking about in this section? (See **Romans 5:14**.)

What entered the world through that man?

Who has sinned according to the end of this verse?

Read **Romans 5:19**. Through Adam's disobedience, many were made what?

This verse in Romans also explains that through Jesus, many will be made righteous. More on that in the next lesson. Let's continue.

Read **Ecclesiastes 7:20**. According to this verse, is anyone free of sin?   Yes   No

Read **Romans 3:9-10** and verse **23**. Who can claim they are righteous besides Jesus?

Also read **Genesis 8:21**. From when are our hearts evil?

Finally, read **Ephesians 2:1-3**. By nature, we are children of what?

Read *Job 15:14-16*. According to verse 16, what two things are people?

Read *1 John 1:8* and *10*. How would you summarize what these verses say?

Although the scribes and Pharisees appeared righteous on the outside, were they righteous? Continue to find out.

Read *Matthew 23:27-28*. What two things were they on the inside?

Before anyone believes in Jesus, they cannot claim to be sinless. We are born into this world and cannot escape sin in our flesh. The good news about this fact is that it doesn't matter how much or how badly we have sinned to be declared unrighteous. It takes the pressure off, like getting the first scratch on your new car, except this is a matter of eternal life or death, not just a matter of vanity. And God does have a way for us to become shiny and new again. Before we talk about that, though, let's look at how rotten our flesh is.

Our Old Man & Woman

When we are born into this fallen world, we are born into our sinful nature, or what is called our *flesh* in the Bible. (*Flesh* also refers to our skin and bones. The context of the writing will determine which *flesh* the Bible is talking about.) That sinful nature is what the apostle Paul sometimes calls the *old man*. As much as I'd like to avoid including women in this lesson, I cannot do that. We ladies have an *old woman*, too.

Let's start by looking at that old self. Who is he or she?

Read *Romans 7:5*. Before being in Christ, to what does our flesh bear fruit?

Read *Romans 7:18*. Paul states that in his flesh, what dwells?

Can Paul find how to perform what is good in his flesh?   Yes   No

Read *Titus 3:3*. List the characteristics of our old self mentioned here by Paul.

Read the second part of *Ephesians 4:22*. (We will get to the first part in a later chapter.)

Our old self grows what?

According to what?

Our old self just gets worse and worse. We can't win that battle no matter how hard we try.

Read *Mark 14:38*. What does Jesus say about the flesh?

Notice and keep in mind that Jesus makes a distinction between the flesh and the spirit.

Read *Philippians 3:3*. We should have no confidence in our what?

Read *John 6:63*. What profit does the flesh offer?

Read *Galatians 5:17*. Who does the flesh lust against?

We see that our flesh, or sinful nature, is weak, corrupt, cannot get any better, is not trustworthy, and it is what fights against the Spirit. That seems bleak. Yes, it is bleak! That is why Jesus came and why we need Him. The good news is that our destiny is not to remain bound by that old man or woman. Jesus came to make us into new men and women. I'll introduce you to that new person in chapter six.

I want to wrap up this lesson by ensuring you understand that everyone is born into sin, and our flesh is capable of doing a lot of unrighteous stuff, but that doesn't mean we only did unrighteous things before we came to Jesus. (See *Luke 6:32-34* for proof.) It simply means that to whatever degree we did righteous things, our righteousness couldn't ever measure up to God's standard. The point is, God is perfectly righteous, and before receiving Jesus' righteousness, we are not.

Why Does it Matter to You?

Why does it matter that you understand and believe that all people are born unrighteous? How might that drive the depth of your understanding of yourself and the Gospel of Grace?

Why it Matters to Grace

I believe it is essential for us to know we are born unrighteous and that we don't become unrighteous through what we do or say. Too often, people who think they are made unrighteous because of their bad behaviors believe they can work to become righteous through their good behaviors. If you know that there is no way in this universe for you to make yourself righteous, then you will give up trying and seek the only way for you to become righteous, which is through faith in Jesus and His assigned righteousness by His radical and astounding grace.

Confirm the Brick

Place a check mark beside it if you believe the following statement is true.

All of humanity is born unrighteous.

Jesus is Our Righteousness
Brick 6

"Now this is His name by which He will be called: THE LORD OUR RIGHTEOUSNESS."

Jeremiah 23:6

Our righteousness is flawed; we have chinks, holes, and cracks. We need the righteousness of God to meet His standard because only His righteousness is perfect. It is for this reason that Jesus came to save us.

The Foundational Truth

Jesus is our righteousness.

In this lesson, we affirm that our righteousness cannot be achieved through our own efforts. It is Jesus, and only Jesus, who is the path to perfect righteousness. In chapter six, we will explore how Jesus accomplishes this, but for now, let's start by understanding how God views our own righteousness.

Our Righteousness

It doesn't matter how hard we try; we cannot make ourselves righteous enough to meet God's standard of perfection.

Read *Isaiah 64:6*. Isaiah tells us that our righteousness is like what?

Do you know that this translation is trying to be polite here? Those rags are menstrual cloths according to the original Hebrew words. Any effort we make to be more righteous is useless because our righteousness is only as good as dirty rags in God's eyes.

Next read *Luke 16:15*. What we might think should be revered or appreciated is what in the sight of God?

Read *Isaiah 57:12*. According to the LORD God, do our own righteousness and works profit us?

Yes   No

Seek Jesus' Righteousness

We can't truly fathom God's righteousness because His definition of righteousness differs greatly from humanity's. Yet, some of us still seek to establish our own righteousness as if we can achieve God-like righteousness. God asks us to seek Him for His righteousness because that is the righteousness that He requires.

Read *Matthew 5:6*. Blessed are whom?

They shall be what?

Read *Matthew 6:33*. What two things are we to seek according to this verse?

Read *Romans 10:3*. What are we to submit to?

Read *Jeremiah 23:5-6*. What is the name that Jeremiah says Jesus will be known by?

Notice it doesn't say Jesus' name is The Righteous Lord, which would have been perfectly correct. Rather, Jeremiah tells us that **Jesus is *our righteousness***. Wow!

Read *Philippians 3:8-9*. Our righteousness is from whom?

Read *2 Corinthians 5:21*. Jesus became sin for us so we could become what?

When we put our faith in Jesus, He gives us **His** righteousness.

Read *Romans 5:19*. By one Man's (Jesus') obedience many will be made what?

Read *Romans 4:5-6*. God imputes what apart from works?

Read *Romans 4:11*. What was imputed?

It is important to remember that the word *impute* here means *to put down to a person's account*. (Vine, Unger, & White, Jr., 1984, 1996, p. 322) Jesus puts His righteousness on our account when we put our faith in Him.

Read *Romans 9:30*. This verse tells us that those who didn't even pursue righteousness, have attained to what?

Read *Romans 5:17*. What gift does this verse mention?

Though we cannot attain perfect righteousness through our efforts, if we put our faith in Jesus' righteousness for our own, we meet God's standard of perfection, which is the only way to do so. This concept is a foundational part of the Gospel of Radical Grace.

Why Does it Matter to You?

Why is it important that you know the only way you can become righteous enough to be with God is through the gift of righteousness that Jesus offers? Does this fact affect your understanding of radical grace?

Why it Matters to Grace

Like what we learned in the previous lesson, knowing we cannot become righteous through our efforts frees us from striving to do so and allows us to rest in the gift that Jesus has given us. Jesus imputes His righteousness to us so He can be with us now and forever. This act of love helps to define what true radical grace is all about.

Confirm the Brick

Place a check next to the sentence below if you believe it is true.

Jesus' gift of perfect righteousness is the only way to meet God's standard.

Build the Foundation of Radical Grace

It is time to cement these bricks called *Righteousness* down into your foundation of radical grace. Righteousness is the main point of the Gospel. Without obtaining Jesus' righteousness through faith in Him, you have no hope and are condemned. The good news of radical grace is our redemption through Jesus and our receiving His imputed righteousness.

Bricks 4, 5, and 6: *Righteousness*

What to know:

God is perfectly righteous and holds us to His standard of righteousness.

We are born into this world unrighteous in our flesh.

By faith in Jesus, we receive His righteousness, which meets God's standard.

Remember, once these bricks are cemented down, you can't move them.

Live Free and Unashamed

We read in Genesis 3 that when the serpent told Eve that she wouldn't die, he incited Eve to distrust and doubt God. His lie ate away at her faith in the LORD God. Deception is a standard play for the devil. If he can create doubt about Jesus, he can lead people away from Him. Have you had, or are you currently having, moments of doubt or mistrust of God? If so, can you pinpoint anything that led to those doubts or may have influenced your disbelief or mistrust of God?

I have witnessed legalistic-leaning people ask questions of others in a similar way to how the serpent did with Eve. They might ask, *"Have you spent enough time in your prayer closet this week?"* or *"Is God okay with what you are doing?"* These condemning questions make the hearer wonder what God thinks of them based on what they have done or not done. Have you ever experienced these types of questions from others? Reflect on how those questions made you feel

I encourage you to stand strong in your faith and don't let anyone lure you away from that confidence. Keep the faith and trust that God loves you always. Don't allow others to make you doubt that truth.

For further insight, read **Romans chapter 5**.

Chapter 3

Promise

"And if you are Christ's, then you are Abraham's seed, and heirs according to the promise."

Galatians 3:29

I f you have kids, you know that if you promise them something, they will hold you to account. If you forget or neglect to fulfill your promise to them, they ensure you understand that *"you promised!"* Like small children, we all understand the concept of a promise. We also understand that if someone breaks a promise to us, it is a form of betrayal. We look for people to have integrity and to keep their word. Sadly, we humans fail at this all the time.

God, however, is the definition of integrity, and He keeps His promises. One such promise is the topic of this chapter. It is the greatest promise ever made, and its fulfillment determines the eternal fate of all who are born into this world.

The next three bricks in the foundation of radical grace are under the heading called *Promise*. These bricks remind us of God's love. His love is so immense that He planned from the foundation of the world to make sure we could be with Him forever. He hinted at it in the Garden of Eden, revealed the promise to Abraham, and fulfilled it through His Son, Jesus.

In this chapter, we discover that since time began, God had a plan in place to bring us back into right standing with Him.

Read chapter 5 of *Radical Grace* if you are reading it with this study.

God Promised Abraham
Brick 7

"And in you all the families of the earth shall be blessed."

Genesis 12:3

Today's lesson profoundly affected my understanding of the Gospel of Grace. Before I understood this promise by God, I was mistaken about the Old Covenant and how I should approach it. I, like many others, would try to mix the Old Covenant and the Law with my New Covenant faith and relationship with Jesus, which only created tremendous confusion, frustration, and shame. Knowing God's promise, the timing of it, and its significance cleared my confusion and eliminated my frustration and shame. It's time for it to do the same for you.

God's heart is filled with a deep longing for all of us to be with Him for eternity. His love for the people He creates is boundless, and He yearns for fellowship with us. Even after sin entered the world through Adam and Eve's disobedience, God's plan to restore our relationship with Him was set in motion.

The Foundational Truth

God promised Abraham that one of his descendants would bless the world.

Today's lesson will teach us about this not-often-discussed yet astonishing promise made thousands of years before Jesus came. He made that promise because He desires our fellowship. God knew the only way we could be in fellowship with Him was through the sacrifice of His Son, Jesus, and His assigning us His righteousness.

God Wants You to Be with Him

The first step in understanding this brick is knowing God wants you to be with Him. His desire for fellowship is why He made the promise to begin with and why He suffered to fulfill it.

Begin by reading *1 John 4:10* and *4:19*. We love Him because He what?

Read *Matthew 18:14*. According to this verse, what is the will of the Father?

Next read *Ezekiel 18:32*. God takes no pleasure in what?

According to the prophet Ezekiel, what are we to do?

Read *1 Timothy 2:3-4*. What is God's desire?

Now read *2 Peter 3:9*. The Lord is not willing that what?

But He wants all to do what?

The Lord is not slack concerning what?

We read that the Lord is not slack concerning His promise, but what was His promise? We examine that next.

God's Promise

The LORD God promised Abraham four things. For clarity, Abraham's name was Abram at the time. God later changed it.

Read *Genesis 12:1*. Notice that the LORD told Abraham to move from Haran. Read *Genesis 12:7*. What was it that the LORD promised Abraham?

Read the first sentence of *Genesis 12:2* and then *Genesis 15:5*. What was the promise the LORD God made to Abraham?

Read the rest of *Genesis 12:2* and *Genesis 24:1*. What did the LORD promise to do for Abraham?

Read *Genesis 12:3*. What does the last line say the LORD promised Abraham?

Abraham went on to live in Canaan. The LORD met with Abraham and explained to him that he would have an heir to inherit all that was promised to him.

Read *Genesis 15:1-6*. (Bonus points for reading all of chapter 15.) What does verse six say?

What did the LORD account Abraham's belief, or faith, for?

Keep this in mind for lesson three of this chapter.

Chapter fifteen of Genesis speaks about a specific heir, or descendant, of Abraham's that would partake in the promises. Who is that heir? Yeah, you probably already know, but in the effort to be thorough, we will find him in the Word.

Read *Genesis 18:10-14* and *Genesis 21:1-3*. What is the name of Abraham's son?

Isaac is Abraham's son and is the ancestor of the one who fulfilled the LORD's promise. We will return to Abraham's heir, Isaac, in lesson two. To show you that Jesus is a descendant of Abraham and Isaac, let's look at Jesus' genealogy.

Read *Matthew 1:1-16* and *Luke 3:23-38*. Notice the genealogy in Matthew says Jesus is descended from David's son Solomon (verse 6), and in Luke it says Jesus is descended from David's son Nathan (verse 31). It is common thought that the list in Matthew follows Joseph's genealogy and the list in Luke is Mary's, but the point is that Jesus is a direct descendant of Abraham.

Today, we discovered four promises the LORD made to Abraham. The first three promises the LORD made were specific to Abraham and his descendants, the future nation of Israel. God promised Abraham land and numerous descendants and that He would bless him and his family. However, the fourth part of the promise is most significant to you and me. Note the promise I want you to know and cement down in your foundation of radical grace: God told Abraham that all the world would be blessed through him and his seed.

How will everyone be blessed? What exactly is this promise? The promised blessing is the New Covenant Gospel of Radical Grace. Jesus is the embodiment of this promised blessing, and He is the good news of God's grace. The Gospel of Grace is the New Covenant God made with humanity. It was a new covenant, but it wasn't a new idea for God. Before we conclude this lesson, let's examine two more passages that unveil the idea that God's plan was in place since before time began.

Read *2 Timothy 1:8-10*. When does verse 9 say His own purpose and grace was given to us in Christ?

Read *Revelation 13:8*. When does this verse say Jesus, the Lamb of God, was slain?

God revealed His plan to Abraham through His promise to him and his descendants, but He had this plan in mind since the beginning. Jesus' mission was never an afterthought.

The blessings of the promise of the Gospel of Grace are many. The following list shows some fundamental blessings of putting your faith in Jesus and His righteousness. I provide one scripture reference for each item on the list here but you can find many more within the pages of the Bible.

In Christ, we are:

Forgiven (*Ephesians 1:7*)
Brought near to God (*Ephesians 2:13*)
Made new by the Spirit (*2 Corinthians 5:17*)
Made righteous (*Romans 9:30*)
Made holy (*Ephesians 4:24*)
Made free from the bondage of the Law (*Romans 8:2*)
Made free from the bondage of sin (*Romans 6:22*)
Given eternal life (*John 3:15*)
Given all the spiritual blessings in the heavenly places (*Ephesians 1:3*)
Given the Holy Spirit to live with us (*Ephesians 1:13*)

This list is worth celebrating! Jesus fulfilled the LORD's promise to Abraham, and He offers these blessings to those who believe that He is who fulfilled the promise. Wow!

Why Does it Matter to You?

Why is it crucial for you to understand that God had a plan since the beginning of time to send Jesus to save the world? How does this timing affect your perspective on the Gospel and God's grace?

Why it Matters to Grace

This promise matters because we can see the heart of God in it. It reminds us that God is gracious, loving, and unwilling that anyone should be separated from Him. He promised to make a way for all to come to Him, even though we are born estranged from Him. He knew from the start that we would fail and not be able to be perfectly righteous by our efforts, so He made this plan to give us His righteousness if we have faith in Him. This promise is a banner for His radical grace.

Confirm the Brick

Do you believe that God promised Abraham that one of his descendants would bless the world? If so, place a check next to the following statement.

God promised Abraham that one of his descendants would bless the world.

Jesus is the Seed of Abraham
Brick 8

"Now to Abraham and His Seed were the promises made. He does not say,
'And to seeds,' as of many, but as of one, 'And to your Seed,' who is Christ."

Galatians 3:16

We can see God's promise threaded through time, starting in the Garden of Eden, weaving through the lives of Abraham, Isaac, Jacob, and King David, and being fulfilled by their descendant, Jesus. A key to studying this promise is to follow the promised Seed throughout the Bible.

The Foundational Truth

Jesus is the promised Seed.

God told the serpent in the garden that He would put enmity between his seed, meaning his followers, and her Seed, meaning the One descended from the woman. Abraham descended from Adam and Eve through their son Seth. Through Abraham's son, Isaac, Jacob was born. Jacob, whose name God changed to Israel (***Genesis 32:28***), had twelve sons with many descendants. King David descended from Jacob through Jacob's son Judah. We can follow the thread of the seed through this genealogy to confirm that Jesus is the Seed of Abraham, promised by the LORD God.

God Promised a Seed

God hinted at His future promise to Abraham in the punishment He gave to Eve after she and Adam ate the forbidden fruit. He had this plan in mind while disciplining Adam, Eve, and the serpent for their sin in the garden. In fact, the apostle John tells us that this planned promise was in His mind from the foundation of the world, as we read in lesson one.

Read *Genesis 3:15*. The LORD told the serpent there would be enmity between him and the woman. Interestingly, He didn't say between the serpent and Adam. Why do you suppose this is?

The LORD told the serpent that the enmity would be between his seed and her Seed. A tree bears fruit, and inside that fruit is a seed that grows more fruit when planted, right? This process is the science of producing offspring. Interestingly, though, in people, the man carries the seed when producing offspring, not the woman. We mustn't miss the distinction God made about the seed. The LORD was giving us a hint at the future person who would become the fulfillment of His promise.

Adam and Eve had offspring, who had children, who had more children, and so on. We can follow their genealogies to Mary and Jesus (See *Luke 3:23-38*). However, when it comes to Jesus, Mary is His mother, but who is His father? **Read *Luke 1:26-35*** for the answer.

Also read *Isaiah 7:14* and *Galatians 4:4*. These verses only mention that Jesus was born of a woman, they do not mention a man. Given these scriptures, what do you think the LORD foreshadowed in His punishment of Eve and what is the significance of this revelation?

Next, we will explore the Seed promised through Abraham, Isaac, and Jacob. As we go through this lesson, take note of the consistency of the term seed that God uses.

Read *Genesis 21:8-12*. Which of Abraham's sons did the LORD say he will call?

Now read *Genesis 22:1-19*. What did the LORD say to Abraham in verse 18?

Knowing that Isaac was the promised heir, Abraham must have been a little confused when the LORD asked him to sacrifice him on an altar. We can discover some interesting insight to what Abraham must have been thinking from the book of Hebrews.

Read *Hebrews 11:17-19*. What does the writer of Hebrews suggest Abraham believed about this request from God?

I'd like to take a moment to cover something that is both fascinating and wonderful that relates to this event involving Isaac.

Read *Hebrews 11:19* again. It states that Abraham received Isaac from the dead, meaning in a figurative sense. Before reading on, think about what that might suggest.

In Abraham's mind, from the time the LORD asked him to sacrifice his son until the moment the angel stopped him, Isaac was as good as dead. I'm sure Abraham was relieved when the LORD provided a ram for the offering instead. Therefore, Abraham received Isaac back from the dead figuratively, not literally, since he never died. Interestingly, *Genesis 22:4* says Abraham offered his son three days after God asked him to make the offering. Those three days symbolize Jesus's three days in the tomb, and God received His Son back from the dead (See *Matthew 12:40*).

In a literal sense, God waited three days to receive His Son, Jesus, back from the dead after His death on the cross. However, God also experienced a period, like Abraham, when He knew Jesus was going to die. God knew of His Son's future death thousands of years before He was crucified. Let's look at this, as it is important to grasp the timing of God's plan to save us.

Read *1 Peter 1:20*. This verse says Jesus' sacrifice was foreordained before when?

God had this planned promise in mind since the beginning.

This idea is a little confusing since, as we understand time, Jesus' death wasn't until many thousands of years after creation or the foundation of the world. Like Abraham, God has had His Son's death in mind, but for a much longer time. God knew about His Son's death since the foundation of the world, but even so, He loves us so much that He didn't create us without having this plan to save us.

God knew what Adam and Eve would do. God knew we would need a Savior. God promised Abraham that He would provide that Savior and He told Abraham's descendants He would keep His promise.

Next read *Genesis 26:1-5*. What did the LORD say to Isaac?

Read *Genesis 28:10-14*. Who did the LORD reiterate His promise to in this passage?

Jesus is the Seed

We know that the LORD God promised that a descendant, or seed, of Abraham, Isaac, and Jacob would bless all the families of the world. Who is the Seed? Let's follow the thread of this promised Seed that is woven through the life of King David, who is a descendant of Abraham through Jacob.

Read *2 Timothy 2:8*, *Romans 1:1-4*, and *Acts 13:21-23*. Do these verses link King David to Jesus, and Jesus to the promise?　　　Yes　　　No

Read *Acts 3:22-26*. Who does Peter say is the one who fulfilled God's promise?

Now read *Galatians 3:16*. Who does Paul say is the promised Seed?

Bonus reading: *Isaiah chapter 53*.

We learn that Jesus is the Seed. Jesus is a direct descendant of Eve through Abraham, Isaac, Jacob, and King David. He is the promised Savior of the Gospel of Grace. What a blessing that God had a plan in mind since before sin entered the world. He would send His Son to bless the world by dying to take away their sin and give them new life in Him. This promise and its fulfillment is the New Covenant that God made with those of us who put our faith in Jesus.

Why Does It Matter to You?

Why does it matter that you believe that Jesus is the Seed, or descendant, of Abraham? How would it affect the Gospel of Grace if Jesus wasn't the promised Seed?

Why it Matters to Grace

Once I understood God's promise to Abraham, I saw God in a whole different light. For most of my life, I pictured God always judging me and being disappointed in me. Knowing that He had this plan in mind because He knows I am sinful helped me to understand that He is a loving and gracious God. He had already set Jesus' sacrificial death and resurrection on the calendar since the beginning of time. He knows we are born into sin, but because He wants us to be with Him, He planned and promised to give us a way back. This promise to send His Son to save those who put their faith in Him is the epitome of His radical grace.

Confirm the Brick

Are you convinced that according to the Bible, Jesus is the promised seed of Abraham? If so, put a check next to the statement below.

Yes, Jesus is the promised Seed.

Promise of Faith
Brick 9

"For the promise that he would be the heir of the world was not to Abraham or to his seed through the law, but through the righteousness of faith."

Romans 4:13

God did not predicate the coming of the promised Savior on our doing anything. He promised a Savior to bless the world, and He delivered on that promise whether we believe that to be true or whether we receive the benefits of it or not. It's a done deal. The ball is now in our court. We can only participate in that promised New Covenant and receive the blessings if we have faith that these things are true. We must believe that Jesus is the fulfillment of God's promise of the New Covenant and that He is the good news of His grace.

The Foundational Truth

The promised New Covenant is received by faith and faith alone.

Today's lesson teaches us that we receive the promised New Covenant Gospel by faith and faith alone. Abraham received the promise, and because of his faith, God made him righteous. We partake in God's promise of blessing when we put our faith in Jesus. We also note that though God gave the Jewish nation the Law well after He made the promise, the Law did not annul the previously given promise. Additionally, we begin the exploration of the relationship that faith and grace have with works and the Law but will revisit this relationship in later chapters as well.

Abraham's Faith

God promised Abraham he would have a descendant who would bless the world. When Abraham believed God, He gave Abraham the gift of righteousness because of his great faith. Like Abraham, it is our faith, not our works, that gives us access to God's promises of righteousness and grace.

Read **Romans 4:1-4**. What does Paul say in verse 2 that Abraham could do if he was justified by his works?

Paul goes on to say that if one works, his or her wages are counted as debt, not what?

Next read **Romans 11:6**. This is an interesting verse placed amidst Paul speaking about a remnant of Israel that will come to the Father through His grace. It is worth noting because Paul clarifies salvation is by grace and not by what?

Paul tells us that grace isn't grace unless it is one hundred percent grace. If we think that our works play any role in our standing with God, then our works would be counted as God's debt. He doesn't owe us salvation because we might do good works or obey the Jewish Law. If we think He does, we take His grace in vain, and then grace is not grace. Also, we could and would boast about our participation in obtaining our salvation and holiness. We do not receive the promise through our works of the Law or any other attempt at good works. We may only receive it by faith through His grace. Our works don't have the power to compel God to give us mercy or favor.

Chapter four in Romans beautifully describes that Abraham received the promise of God, believed Him, and because of his faith, he was made righteous. It explains that, in Christ, we are considered his heirs who inherit the spoils of that promise through our faith.

Return to **Romans 4:3**. Because Abraham believed God, what was accounted to him?

The word *accounted* here means the same as *imputed* which we talked about in chapter two, *Righteousness*.

Now read **Romans 4:5-8**. What does verse 5 say faith is accounted for?

And who is it accounted to?

Read *Romans 4:9-12*. Note verse 11. Who is Abraham the father of?

Furthermore, what is imputed, or given to his children?

Read *Romans 4:13-16*. According to verse 13, was the promise made through the Law or through the righteousness of faith?   Law   Faith

What does verse 14 say? What happens to faith and the promise if we think we are heirs of God through the Law?

Now read *Romans 4:17-18*. God told Abraham he would be the father to many nations and descendants. Who are those people according to this section of Romans 4?

It is true that Abraham is the father of a large nation called Israel, but he is also the father of all of us who come to Jesus by faith (See *Romans 9:6-8*).

Read *Romans 4:19-22*. Again, why was Abraham accounted as righteous?

Next read *Romans 4:23-25*. What do we who believe receive?

Why was Jesus delivered up?

And why was He raised?

Read *Galatians 3:5-9*. Who does Paul say can be sons of Abraham?

Note that this passage says that the promise Abraham was given is indeed the gospel.

Next read *Ephesians 2:4-7*. What does verse 5 say we are saved by?

Read *Ephesians 2:8-9*. Verse 8 says we are saved by *grace*, what does it say we are saved *through*?

Grace and faith are partners. God gives grace; we receive it through our faith in Jesus.

Paul clarifies the relationship between grace and works. How would you describe that relationship according to this passage?

Bonus reading: *Ephesians 2:11-22*.

The Promise Preceded the Law

Romans chapter four makes it clear that the promise of the Gospel was not about obedience to the Law. In fact, as we just read, the promise of the Gospel was given to Abraham well before God gave Moses the Law.

Read *Galatians 3:15-18*. According to verse 17, how many years after God promised Abraham did God give the Law to the nation of Israel?

This passage states that the Law, which came centuries after the covenant God made with Abraham, cannot annul, or terminate, that deal. Inheritance cannot be of promise if it is of what?

The promised Gospel precedes and supersedes the Law.

Next, we examine another section in the Bible to clarify the distinction between the promised Gospel and the Law.

Read *Galatians 4:21-5:1*. Who are the two sons mentioned in verse 22? (See *Genesis 16:1*, *16:15*, and *17:19*.)

Note *Galatians 4:23-26*. This passage says that one son, referring to Ishmael, was born of the flesh, and the other son, Isaac, was born of the promise. According to this passage, why are they distinguished this way? (See also *Genesis 21:10* and *Exodus 31:18*.)

Who does *Galatians 4:28* say we are?

Read *Galatians 4:30*. Paul references this passage from Genesis.

Lastly, *Galatians 4:31* says we are not children of the bondwoman, but of the free. What does this mean?

The Bible clarifies for us that the promised Gospel is all about faith and not the Law. All the blessings of the promise come to us not through our works of the Law or obedience to good works, but through God's grace by our faith in Christ.

Bonus reading: Read *Luke 1:46-55* in which Mary, the mother of Jesus, worshipped God, and *Luke 1:67-75* in which the priest and father of John the baptizer, Zacharias, also worshipped God. Both glorified God for the coming Savior.

Why Does it Matter to You?

Why does it matter that you believe the promise is by faith and faith alone? How does this question get to the heart of what grace is?

Why it Matters to Grace

If salvation came by anything other than faith through grace, we would have to work to receive it. The fact that Abraham received righteousness by faith is the very definition of grace. People who believe we are to work for our membership in the New Covenant and the blessing of righteousness are walking away from His grace and drowning themselves in legalism. However, knowing the truth of this lesson keeps us in His grace and living our lives in the freedom and blessings that He has given us.

Confirm the Brick

Do you believe that you receive God's promised New Covenant simply by putting your faith in Jesus? If your answer is yes, put a check mark next to the statement.

Yes, I receive the promised New Covenant by faith and faith alone.

Build the Foundation of Radical Grace

These *Promise* bricks can now be cemented down into your foundation of radical grace. It is imperative that you know God had a plan to save you since the beginning. Knowing about His promise helps you grasp His great love for you and the beauty of His radical grace.

Bricks 7, 8, and 9: *Promise*

What to know:

God promised Abraham a future Savior because He wants to be with you forever.

Jesus is the promised Seed of Abraham and Savior who ushered in the promised New Covenant.

The promise is by grace through faith and faith alone. It is not by obedience to the Law.

Remember, once you place these bricks you can't remove them.

Live Free and Unashamed

Can you imagine being asked by God to sacrifice your child or any loved one on an altar? I admit I have difficulty imagining how I would feel in that situation. It must have been excruciating for Abraham to do what the LORD God asked of him. However, we learn in Hebrews that Abraham had faith that God would make it all okay, even if that meant He would raise Isaac from the dead. And because Abraham was faithful, God blessed him with His righteousness.

Life on this planet can be difficult. On any given day, it might not be as bad as sacrificing your child, but things can certainly be challenging. This week, hold dear to the concept that you are a child of God through His grace by your faith and faith alone. You don't need to work hard to get God's attention to help you when things are tough. He is with you on both the good and bad days.

Also, know and act with that knowledge that God has a plan for your life. Abraham couldn't see the complete picture of his trip up the mountain with his son, but He trusted God to get him through to the trip down. Whatever mountains you are facing today, trust God and have faith that He has you in His loving arms.

For more information, read ***Romans chapter 4***.

Old Covenant

"Moreover the law entered that the offense might abound.
But where sin abounded, grace abounded much more"

Romans 5:20

Have you ever questioned your relationship with the Old Covenant as a New Covenant believer? Does God require you to try to fulfill the old Law? If so, which ones of the 613 documented in our Bibles? Many in our Christian community place great importance on the Ten Commandments but don't mention the other 603. This lack of clarity about our obedience to the Old Covenant Law creates needless confusion. However, this chapter is here to bring clarity and resolve this confusion.

The Old Covenant is necessary to understand because it plays a vital role in contrasting the New Covenant and helping us comprehend it. We cannot understand the new deal of grace unless we understand what life would have been like without it. That contrast aids in our acceptance of and realization of the powerful and overwhelming gift that Jesus has given us through His death and resurrection.

Because our Christian leaders do not often distinguish the Old Covenant from the New Covenant in their messaging, they create a foggy bridge between the two. This clouded view of the covenants causes believers to be uncertain about whether they are supposed to traverse back and forth across that bridge or not.

Through the study of these *Old Covenant* bricks, we not only lift the fog from this topic, but we will remove the bridge altogether as we examine the Old Covenant, its purpose, and its position with the followers of Christ.

Read chapter 6 of *Radical Grace* if you are reading it with this study.

Israel Couldn't Obey the Law
Brick 10

"Now therefore, if you will indeed obey My voice and keep My covenant,
then you shall be a special treasure to Me above all people; for all the earth is Mine."

Exodus 19:5

The LORD God gave His Law to Moses from atop Mt. Sinai to pass along to the nation of Israel. God's covenant, or deal with the Jewish people, was conditional and based on their obedience to His Law. Their obedience or disobedience would determine either their blessing or their punishment. We can learn much from the history of the nation of Israel regarding their obedience to God's Law

The Foundational Truth

Israel could not obey the Law of Moses, and we cannot either.

This lesson's basis is that Israel failed to be perfectly obedient to the LORD God and to the Law, which He gave them through Moses. Understanding their failure will help us understand our relationship to the Law as New Covenant believers.

Before we can fully grasp our relationship to the Law, we, as New Covenant believers, must delve into the covenant, or contract, that God had with the Jewish nation. This understanding is a crucial steppingstone in our journey to comprehend our responsibility to the Old Covenant Law.

The Old Covenant

We can see that the Old Covenant was a conditional covenant by the fact that it includes the words *if* and *then*.

Read *Exodus 19:5-6*. Notice the words *if* and *then*. What is the *if* part? What is the *then* part?

List the three things God would do for the Israel nation if they kept His covenant.

Read *Exodus 23:20-22 & 25-26*. Notice the other blessings if the nation obeyed.

Read *Exodus 24:7-8*. What did the Jewish nation say they would do?

The Old Covenant was a conditional, or a two-way covenant. Both parties to the agreement have conditions that they must meet. We have read about what the LORD God would do if they obeyed, but what was the nation's requirement as a participant in this agreement? They were required to follow God's Law.

The Old Testament contains and explains the Old Covenant Law. We can read the entire volume of the Law, which consists of 613 laws, in the books of Exodus, Leviticus, Numbers, and Deuteronomy. The following is a sampling of three of these 613 Mosaic laws.

Read *Deuteronomy 23:19*. What can they not charge their brother according to the Mosaic Law?

According to *Deuteronomy 23:24*, can they take a bag of grapes from their neighbor's vineyard?

Yes   No

Now read *Deuteronomy 24:19*. What must they do if they forget to load up all their sheaves of grain in the wagon?

There are 610 other laws listed in the Old Testament. The LORD God gave Moses ten of those laws written on stone tablets while atop Mt. Sinai. It is time to brush up on our Ten Commandments.

Read *Exodus 20:1-17*. List the ten laws that God gave the nation of Israel on the stone tablets.

For more understanding, you may want to read *Deuteronomy 28*.

Did the Jewish nation obey the Ten Commandments and the list of over 600 more? Let's find out if they met the requirements to fulfill the covenant.

Israel's Disobedience

If you have read the Old Testament, you know Israel struggled many times to observe God's covenant with them. At times, they did repent and get back on track, but the fact remains that they couldn't perfectly obey the Law God gave them, and when they didn't, they suffered the consequences.

We can read about one such time they turned away from the LORD in *Exodus 32*. What did they do in this chapter that went against God?

Read *Jeremiah 11:1-10*. According to this passage, did the people who lived at the time of Jeremiah's prophecy obey the LORD?   Yes   No

Read *Acts 15:6-10*. Who is Peter referring to as *us* and *them* in verse 9?

What is the *yoke* Peter is talking about in verse 10?

What does Peter mean by saying, *"...neither our fathers nor we were able to bear"*?

Read *Acts 15:11*. In what manner will the Jewish people and the Gentiles be saved?

The Jewish nation could not obey God's Law all the time. Peter knew this and admitted that he and his peers couldn't do it either. We benefit from looking at this history and realizing we would not have obeyed the Law perfectly. We can't, but Jesus did, which was part of His mission when He came.

So, why did God give the Law to the Jewish nation if He knew they couldn't obey it? We will examine the answer to that question in the next lesson.

Why Does it Matter to You?

How does Israel's failure to obey the Law perfectly affect your understanding of your ability to follow God's Law? How might that help you in your understanding of the Gospel of Radical Grace?

Why it Matters to Grace

As we look at Israel's history, it speaks volumes to us. They struggled to obey the Law perfectly. This disobedience should come as no surprise because of the bricks we have already placed in our foundation under the heading *Righteousness*. As we accept that we are no different than the Israelites, we are humbled by what Jesus has done for us. This chapter's discussion is one of the reasons we needed to place the *Righteousness* bricks into our foundation. We must see the facts about Israel's inability to obey the Mosaic Law so that we can both understand and accept our inability as well. Additionally, we know the reason that Jesus came to usher in the New Covenant and the Gospel of Radical Grace.

Confirm the Brick

Israel failed to hold up their end of the agreement they had with the LORD God. You or I wouldn't have been able to either. Will you take it as truth that Israel's failure to obey speaks to the truth that you and I are right there with them? Place a check mark next to it if you agree with the following statement.

Israel could not completely obey the Law of Moses, and I cannot either.

The Purpose of the Law
Brick 11

"Therefore by the deeds of the law no flesh will be justified in His sight,
for by the law is the knowledge of sin."

Romans 3:20

We cannot cement the *Old Covenant* bricks in place until we understand the purpose of the Law for New Covenant believers. Only then can we see why these bricks are part of our foundation of radical grace. We will discover that the purpose of the Law was not to make us righteous but to teach us about our unrighteousness and, therefore, our need for Jesus.

The Foundational Truth

The Law cannot make one righteous; it makes sin known.

Often, teachers state that it is our duty as believers to fulfill the Old Covenant Law to become righteous, holy, or more Christlike. As we learned in lesson one, *Israel Couldn't Obey the Law*, we can't satisfy the Law perfectly, so we could never meet these goals no matter our effort. However, even if we do a good job of obeying the Law, we can never become righteous through that obedience. I say that boldly because that is what the Word tells us. As we delve into today's lesson, let's remember this fundamental truth: the Law's purpose is not to make us righteous. Its true function for us is to reveal our sinful nature.

The Law Cannot Produce Perfect Righteousness

The Law, no matter how well one obeys it, cannot take away sins, and it cannot make people perfectly righteous. Let's look at what the Word says about this fact.

Read *Galatians 2:21*. Christ would have died in vain if righteousness came how?

Note what Paul says in the first half of this verse. He is unwilling to set aside the grace of God by rejecting Jesus and going back under the Law, seeking to gain his righteousness from trying to obey it. What does this verse imply about the relationship between the Law and grace?

Read *Hebrews 10:1*. What do you think the writer of Hebrews means when he says the Law has a shadow of things, but not the very image?

According to this verse, what can the Law not do?

We will discuss verses 2 and 3 in the next section, but for now, read *Hebrews 10:4*. It is impossible for the blood of bulls and goats to do what?

Read *Philippians 3:8-9*. This verse says that if you are striving to fulfill the Law, you are striving to gain your own what?

How does Paul say he has gained righteousness? From whom and by what?

Read *Romans 10:1-4*. Israel was seeking to gain their righteousness through obedience to the Law. Who ended obedience to the Law for righteousness?

We have learned that the Law cannot make anyone righteous, so what was God's purpose in giving Israel the Law? We will address this question further in lesson three, but first, we will look at how the law reveals the truth about sin.

Purpose of the Law

Read **Hebrews 10:1-2**. This passage explains that if the Law had made people perfect, they wouldn't have had to come year after year to offer sacrifices for their sins.

Once people were cleansed of their sins, they would have had no more consciousness of what?

Think about the magnitude of what this is saying as it relates to followers of Jesus. Believers in Jesus *have been* cleansed of their sin. What might this indicate for the consciousness of the faithful?

Back to those under the Law. Read **Hebrews 10:3**. For those who were under the Law, what were they reminded of every year?

Read **Romans 3:20**. First, we cannot be justified or made righteous, by what?

Second, what does it say the Law does for us?

Read **Romans 5:19-20**. Let's step through this. By Adam's disobedience, many were made what?

By Jesus' obedience, many will be made what?

In the middle of these two events, or men, Adam and Jesus, God gave the Law. What does verse 20 say was the reason?

Next read **Romans 7:7**. How do we know sin?

Read **Romans 7:8-12**. How did sin revive?

Read **Romans 7:13**. Sin through the commandment became what?

God never intended for the Old Covenant Law to be the means to gain righteousness. On the contrary, its purpose was to show us how truly evil our sin is and that we cannot obtain righteousness through our own fleshly works and striving for obedience.

Why Does it Matter to You?

Why is it essential that you understand the purpose of the Law? Does defining its New Covenant purpose change your understanding about your ability to become righteous through your own efforts?

Why it Matters to Grace

God's intention in giving the Law to Israel was to provide a mirror, a measuring stick, for them to recognize their sinfulness. This mirror, however, is not limited to them. It also reflects our own struggles, showing us our need for Jesus in a profound way.

There is something else that the Law has done for us. The last sentence of **Romans 5:20** says that where sin abounded, grace abounded much more. The more we realize the magnitude and unrighteousness of our sinful state, the more we recognize the beauty and love wrapped up in God's radical grace.

Confirm the Brick

The Bible clarifies that we cannot become righteous by obeying the Law. However, the Law did show us that we are unrighteous and sinful. Do you agree with the following statement? If so, put a check mark next to the statement below and hold that truth securely as you continue in this study.

The Law cannot make one righteous, rather, it makes sin known.

Christ is the End of the Law
Brick 12

"For Christ is the end of the law for righteousness to everyone who believes."

Romans 10:4

We must distinguish the details, differences, and dispensations of the two covenants so that we may rightly apply that knowledge to our faith and relationship with Jesus. You might be wondering if God expects you to continue to try to obey the Old Covenant Law. Innumerable teachings contradict each other, considering this topic. Wouldn't it be great to finally understand this issue, cement your understanding into your foundation of radical grace and understanding of the Gospel, and not ever wonder or waver again? Let's do that.

The Foundational Truth

Christ is the end of the Law for righteousness.

Today's foundational truth is vital to understanding the Gospel of Radical Grace. If this statement is accurate, we can truly live free and unashamed.

In his letter to the Galatians, Paul gives us a profound lesson in understanding the difference between the Old Covenant Law and the New Covenant of Jesus, which is all about our faith and God's grace. This lesson, found in Galatians chapter three, is a crucial part of our understanding. We discuss that our righteousness comes by faith and cannot be obtained by obedience to the Law. We also look at the fact that the Law did not cancel the promised deal God made with Abraham and his descendants. And finally, we see that Jesus, as the promised child of Abraham, brought an end to the Old Covenant Law, initiating the New Covenant of faith. Our righteousness is not earned through obedience to the Law but received from our Lord, Jesus.

The Law vs. Faith

In chapter three of the book of Galatians, Paul contrasts the Law with faith. He talks about receiving the Spirit by faith versus receiving Him by obedience to the Law. Receiving the Spirit is akin to our acceptance of the Lord Jesus, or what some might call being saved, because once we receive Jesus, we are born in the Spirit (*John 3:5*), baptized with the Holy Spirit (*Mark 1:8*), and receive Him as a guarantee of our salvation (*2 Corinthians 5:5*).

Read *Galatians 3:1-2*. Do we receive the Spirit because we obey the Law, or because we have faith in Jesus?   Law   Faith

Read *Galatians 3:3*. When we put our faith in Jesus and receive the Spirit, this is a spiritual, rather than fleshly or carnal, activity. Paul asks the Galatians if they think they can be perfected by their fleshly works. This is a rhetorical question, of course, that we should know how to answer.

Sometimes it is helpful to read in other translations. See this verse as it is translated in the New Living Translation.

"How foolish can you be? After starting your Christian lives in the Spirit, why are you now trying to become perfect by your own human effort?"

Galatians 3:3 NLT

Notice that Paul defines works of the flesh as works of the law. Please don't miss this crucial point: the relationship between the flesh and the Law. As you read Paul's epistles, you can see that he equates striving to obey the Law with works of the flesh.

Galatians 3:4 speaks to the Galatians' suffering from their community because they became followers of Jesus. Paul makes the point that their suffering would have been for nothing if they didn't continue to walk by faith but instead returned to living under the Law of Judaism.

Read *Galatians 3:5-7*. Who are considered the sons of Abraham?

Read *Galatians 3:8-9*. The Gentiles are justified by what?

According to these verses, Abraham received the gospel when God made His promise to him. So, those who are of faith are what?

Continuing, read *Galatians 3:10*. Paul shares a quote from *Deuteronomy 27:26*. This verse indicates that if one is to live by the Law, he or she must obey every single law or what happens?

Read *Galatians 3:11*. I am sure you are familiar with the verse Paul references here from *Habakkuk 2:4*. According to this verse we are justified and live by what?

I like how the NLT states this verse.

"So it is clear that no one can be made right with God by trying to keep the law. For the Scriptures say, 'It is through faith that a righteous person has life.'"

Galatians 3:11 NLT

Read *Galatians 3:12*. Paul emphasizes the idea that if you live by the Old Covenant Law and commandments, you must do so fully. You can't have one foot in the Law and the other foot in faith because the Law is not what?

Read *Galatians 3:13-14*. Jesus redeemed us from the curse of the Law, but we may only receive that blessing through the promise of the Spirit through what?

Read *Galatians 3:15-16*. Paul references *Genesis 3:15* and the promise He made to Abraham several times throughout Genesis. Who is the promised descendant and Seed of Abraham?

Read *Galatians 3:17*, which is a jewel of a verse. Paul makes the point that the Law, which the LORD gave over 400 years after He gave Abraham His promise, cannot annul that promised covenant. Read this verse in the NLT.

"This is what I am trying to say: The agreement God made with Abraham could not be canceled 430 years later when God gave the law to Moses. God would be breaking his promise."

Galatians 3:17 NLT

Next read **Galatians 3:18**. Paul gives us a *does not equal* sign here. If *the inheritance = the law*, then *the inheritance ≠ the promise*. Our inheritance does not come by the Law. Our inheritance is by what?

The End of the Law

Next, we examine the last section of Galatians chapter three. Paul explains to us that the Law was given to guard people for a certain period, but that once Jesus came, it was not meant to remain as our guardian.

Read **Galatians 3:19**. Also read it here from the New Living Translation.

"Why, then, was the law given? It was given alongside the promise to show people their sins. But the law was designed to last only until the coming of the child who was promised."

Galatians 3:19 NLT

According to this verse, why was the Law added?

And it was added until when?

Read **Galatians 3:20-22**. Paul is setting up his argument that the Law couldn't give life because it couldn't make anyone righteous. However, the Law reveals to us that we are all under sin. The promise by faith is given to whom?

Read **Galatians 3:23**. Before Jesus, and therefore faith, came, what did the Law do for us?

And it kept us under guard until what?

Read *Galatians 3:24-25*. I've included the NLT for more depth.

"Let me put it another way. The law was our guardian until Christ came; it protected us until we could be made right with God through faith. And now that the way of faith has come, we no longer need the law as our guardian."

Galatians 3:24-25 NLT

The Law was our tutor, schoolmaster, or guardian, to do what?

So that we might be justified by what?

And now that faith has come, we are no longer what?

Finally, read *Galatians 3:26-29*. Those of faith are all one in Christ and we are Abraham's what?

According to what?

There are a few more verses that I'd like you to look at before we move on to the next chapter. These scriptures speak of Jesus bringing an end to the Old Covenant Law for those who are in Him.

Read *Luke 16:16*. Jesus said the law and prophets were until John the baptizer, and since that time, what has been preached?

Read *Hebrews 8:7-13*.

Read *Romans 4:13-14*. The promise was not to Abraham through the Law, but through what?

Bonus points for reading all of *Romans 4*.

Read **Romans 10:4**. Christ is the end of what?

Those who believe are made what?

How did Jesus wipe out the handwriting of requirements (the Law) that was against us? Read **Colossians 2:13-14** for the answer.

Why Does it Matter to You?

Why does it matter that Jesus ended people's required obedience to the Old Covenant Law? What does it change in your life knowing that you are freed from trying to obey the Law to gain your righteousness?

Why it Matters to Grace

Once we give ourselves to the Lord and are members of the New Covenant, we are not required to fulfill the Law because Jesus fulfilled it for us. Knowing this is true helps define our relationship and responsibility as children of God. It also magnifies His grace toward us and highlights that we may rest in that grace from dead works. Being freed from the legalistic venture to fulfill the Old Covenant Law is the very definition of God's radical grace.

Confirm the Brick

Do you see and believe that Jesus came to end the Old Covenant Law for those who believe in Him for their righteousness? If so, put a check mark next to the following foundational statement, and don't waver in your thinking again. Stand confident in your understanding that you are not required to fulfill the Old Covenant or strive to become righteous by your own efforts.

Yes, Christ is the end of the Law for righteousness.

Build the Foundation of Radical Grace

It is time to cement these *Old Covenant* bricks into your definition of God's radical grace to remain confident about the purpose and your relationship to the Law. Jesus put an end to the Old Covenant so He could bring in the New Covenant of grace.

Bricks 10, 11, and 12: *Old Covenant*

Israel could not obey the Old Covenant Law of Moses and we could not have either.

The purpose of the Old Covenant Law isn't to make people righteous, it is to draw people to Jesus because it makes sin known.

Jesus came to fulfill and end the Old Covenant so He could launch the New Covenant. Christ is the end of the Law for righteousness.

Remember, once in place, these bricks can't be moved. If you lift these bricks back up and put yourself back under the Law, you are walking away from God's grace (*Galatians 5:4*).

Live Free and Unashamed

It is humbling to realize that centuries of history reveal that humanity can't walk in perfect righteousness and obedience to God without the Spirit. We must be careful not to judge Adam, Eve, or the people we read about in the Old Testament who struggled to obey God's Law. We must be honest with ourselves and admit we would have failed to succeed at that task, too; frankly, we still do. God's grace teaches us that we are no better or worse than anyone else on the planet. We all have failed, so we can't judge others for their failings.

However, when we allow God's radical grace to pour over our own lives and the lives of others, we realize that because of Jesus, we are forgiven, released from the impossible yoke of obeying the Law, and freed to walk in love toward one another.

I encourage you to allow yourself to be okay with knowing you can't follow the Old Covenant Law perfectly. Have grace with yourself and rest in knowing that Jesus has grace with you. He came to bestow His righteousness on you because He loves you and He doesn't require anything from you except that you receive Him as yours. Breathe. Rest. Rejoice!

For further reading on this topic, read *Galatians chapter 4*.

Chapter 5

New Covenant

"In that He says, 'A new covenant,' He has made the first obsolete.
Now what is becoming obsolete and growing old is ready to vanish away."

Hebrews 8:13

The purpose of studying the Old Covenant is to understand its contrast to the New Covenant. The difference is incredible! The New and Old Covenants are not equal but opposite. They are separate, and each has important distinctions. Where the Old Covenant was one of obedience to works of the Law, the New Covenant is one of grace and faith. The Old Covenant taught us about our sin and lack of righteousness, but the New Covenant teaches us about our holiness and righteousness through Jesus. The Old Covenant produces condemnation, but the New Covenant produces new life, spiritual works of love, and salvation. The New Covenant is not only new, but it is also better.

Read chapters 7-10 of *Radical Grace* if you are reading it with this study.

Pre-study Thoughts

We have examined much of the fundamental doctrine that predicts Jesus coming to bring in a New Covenant and supports the reason for His mission. In the next four chapters, we will dig into the New Covenant to better understand what it is, and explore who we are as members of that new deal. What do you see as significant characteristics of the New Covenant?

A Better Covenant
Brick 13

"Behold, the days are coming, says the LORD, when I will make a
new covenant with the house of Israel and the house of Judah..."

Jeremiah 31:31

Jesus' death and resurrection initiated the New Covenant for His followers. This new deal is a better covenant for us than the one God made with Moses and the Jewish nation because God is the only contributor obligated to fulfill any requirements. All we need to do is receive it by faith.

The Foundational Truth

God promised a new and better covenant.

God's promised New Covenant, available to all who put their faith in His Son, is the answer to humanity's predicament. It surpasses the covenant with the Israelites and revolutionizes our relationship with Him, guiding us in His grace each day.

In chapter three, *Promise*, we learned about God's promise to Abraham that a future descendant would bless the entire world. Today's lesson examines that promise He called the New Covenant. We also discuss why the Bible calls the New Covenant a better covenant.

An "I Will" Covenant

We begin our study of this *better covenant* in the book of Jeremiah. Jeremiah was a prophet of the LORD God who lived about six hundred years before Jesus was born. His prophesies about the coming Messiah are beautiful, and one of his prophecies is particularly helpful for us in today's study.

Read *Jeremiah 31:31-32*. The LORD mentions a new covenant and says that it is not according to the covenant He made with the fathers of the tribes of Israel and Judah. According to God here, did they uphold that old covenant?   Yes   No

I'm sure you noticed that this says the LORD will make a covenant with the houses of Israel and Judah. Does that mean that if you aren't Jewish, this new covenant excludes you? We must remember that Jesus is the Jewish Messiah (Savior). However, in this new deal, He also welcomes the Gentiles. Let's take a brief detour to Isaiah to confirm my answer to this question.

Read *Isaiah 42:1*. The LORD is speaking to His Servant, His Elect One. This is Jesus. This verse says He will bring justice to whom?

Now read *Isaiah 42:6*. Praise God for what He says to Jesus here! He tells His Son that He will be what to the Gentiles?

Check out this interesting verse. Read *John 8:12*. What does Jesus call Himself?

We have our answer then. No, if you are not Jewish, you are not excluded from the New Covenant. Jesus came to be a light to the entire world, both the Jewish nation and the Gentiles. Now, let's get back to Jeremiah.

Read *Jeremiah 31:33*. What four things does the LORD say He will do in this new covenant?

Where will God put and write His law?

It's important to remember that God has placed His law in our hearts and minds to guide our conscience and understanding about sin. As we learned in the last chapter, the Spirit uses the Law to draw us to Christ, making us aware of our own sins. Keep in mind that knowing that God's law is in our minds and hearts doesn't mean we are obligated to fulfill the written Jewish Law from the Old Covenant. We cemented those *Old Covenant* bricks down, knowing the Bible says Jesus was the end of the Law for our righteousness. So as partakers of the New Covenant, we do not need to use the Law as guardrails which we must strive to live within, but we may, however, use the Law spiritually, in the newness of the Spirit (**Romans 7:6**), as a compass to direct us toward love and good works.

Read *Jeremiah 31:34*. God will forgive what?

The last part of verse 34 says God will remember their sin no more. I love this statement. It doesn't say He would forget their sins, but that He won't remember them. He has a willful desire not to retain that information. Wow! This is a subtle but powerful distinction.

In chapter four, we learned that the Old Covenant was an if-then, or conditional, covenant; *if* the people of Israel obeyed God's Law, *then* they would receive blessings. And conversely, *if* they didn't obey, *then* they would receive curses.

Notice the words *if* and *then* are not a part of this promise of a new covenant found in Jeremiah.

What two words does the LORD use repeatedly in these verses?

The use of the phrase *I will* and the lack of the words *if* and *then* shows us that God is the only one with something to do concerning this new deal. He has done it all. This New Covenant is something remarkable. It is a one-sided contract that includes requirements for the Lord but not for us. We have nothing to do but put our faith in Jesus.

The prophet Ezekiel also recorded some *I will* statements made by the LORD God. These promises are prophecies of the New Covenant.

Read *Ezekiel 36:25*. What will God do according to this verse?

Read *Ezekiel 36:26*. What will God do for our hearts?

He also says He will give us a new spirit. Note that this does not refer to the Holy Spirit, who indwells the followers of Jesus, as He mentions Him in the next verse. This refers to us being born of the Spirit into a new spiritual nature.

Read the next verse, *Ezekiel 36:27*. The LORD says He will give us His Spirit. This is the promise that Jesus would send His Spirit to live inside of us.

There is no mention of anything we must do in this promised covenant. All we need to do is receive it by faith.

A Better Covenant

This New Covenant is not only new and different, but also better than the old one.

Read **Hebrews 9:11**. The writer of Hebrews is making the case that Jesus is the High Priest of the tabernacle that is spiritual, not the priest of the physical or material tabernacle who had to go in year after year and sacrifice animals for the sins of the nation. The author calls this new tabernacle greater and more perfect, and not made with hands. It is not of this world. Notice how there is a shift from the physical, material, or earthly kingdom that includes obedience to the Law in the flesh, to the spiritual kingdom and spiritual matters.

Read **Hebrews 9:12**. Jesus did not offer the blood of animals, but He offered what?

And what did He obtain by doing so?

Read **Hebrews 9:13-14**. The animal sacrifices purified the flesh of the people so they could be covered for a time, but Jesus' sacrifice cleanses what?

Now read **Hebrews 9:15**. By means of His death, Jesus is the Mediator of what?

This verse says He redeemed the transgressions that were done under the first covenant so that those of us who believe in Him may receive what?

Chapter 8 of Hebrews spells it out quite clearly. Read **Hebrews 8:1-13**. Summarize verse 6.

What is the significance of verse 7?

What has Jesus made obsolete according to verse 13?

Paul makes quite a contrast between the Old Covenant and New Covenant in his letter to the people of Corinth. Let's examine that section of his letter.

Read *2 Corinthians 3:4-5*. First, Paul makes this statement that we are not sufficient in and of ourselves, but our sufficiency is from whom?

Read *2 Corinthians 3:6*. Paul states that God has made His followers sufficient as ministers of the New Covenant. Then he defines this statement further by saying that it is not of the letter but of the spirit. What does he mean by this statement?

He goes on to say the letter does what?

And the Spirit does what?

How does the letter, or written law kill and the Spirit give life?

Read *2 Corinthians 3:7*. Paul is getting quite bold and calling the Law the ministry of death. However, he does say even it is glorious. The Law is holy, after all. Read *Romans 7:9-13*. Paul explains in Romans why in his letter to the Corinthians he calls the Law the ministry of death.

Read *2 Corinthians 3:8*. If the ministry of death is glorious, wouldn't the ministry of the Spirit be more glorious?   Yes   No

Read *2 Corinthians 3:9*. Here Paul calls the Law the ministry of condemnation and the New Covenant a ministry of righteousness. Why does he call the Law the ministry of condemnation?

Why does he call the New Covenant a ministry of righteousness?

Note that he says the glory of the New Covenant excels, meaning that it excels above, past, and beyond the glory of the Law.

Read *2 Corinthians 3:10*. Now Paul is blatantly saying that because the New Covenant is so glorious, you could say the Law, which God made glorious, had no glory when compared to the new deal.

Finally, read *2 Corinthians 3:11*. Paul sums up his argument in this verse. What does he say is much more glorious?

Why Does it Matter to You?

What does the fact that God provided the New Covenant imply about the Old Covenant? Why would it matter for you to understand that the New Covenant is a better covenant?

Why it Matters to Grace

In the last chapter, we studied the old if-then covenant that God made with the nation of Israel. In today's lesson, we looked at the new deal Jesus brought to the world and the fact that it is an I-will covenant. God executed the conditions and provisions of this new contract. There is nothing we can do to earn our right to this deal except the simple belief that Jesus offers us to participate, that He is who He says He is, and that He did what He said He would do. We put our faith in His righteousness for our own. That's it. That means the New Covenant is a covenant of grace, which is why it is a better deal. If there are requirements that we must fulfill to gain salvation, justification, or sanctification, then the agreement is not one of grace but of works. This new and better covenant reveals God's radical grace.

Confirm the Brick

Do you believe that the promise God made to Abraham was about the New Covenant and that it is a better covenant than the Old Covenant? If so, put a check mark below and forever keep this distinction in your heart and mind.

Yes, God promised a new and better covenant.

Salvation to Believers

Brick: 14

"For I am not ashamed of the gospel of Christ, for it is the power of God to salvation for everyone who believes, for the Jew first and also for the Greek. For in it the righteousness of God is revealed from faith to faith; as it is written, 'The just shall live by faith.'"

Romans 1:16-17

Many religions require their devotees to perform specific duties or rituals, behave in a certain way, or deny themselves particular things. In its pure form (not defiled by man's modification), Christianity has no such requirements. It is about simple belief. We obtain our relationship with God by faith, and we remain in it by faith. If this premise is true, our relationship and salvation are not dependent on our actions or behaviors. We must firmly establish this element of belief in our hearts and minds before we address issues relating to sin, works, obedience, and sanctification.

The Foundational Truth

The New Covenant offers salvation to those who believe.

Our premise in today's study might seem elementary at first, but we must cement this concept in our minds fully, without doubt, to confidently continue our study about grace. We must believe that we are blessed to participate in a covenant with God by our faith, and faith alone. We not only begin there, but because of God's grace, belief is also how we remain and live our lives in relationship with Him. The New Covenant is about faith in all aspects. We get invited to participate if we believe in Jesus' righteousness for our own, and we continue in it by continuing in that belief.

In this lesson, we first delve into the concept that the New Covenant is initiated through belief. Then, we explore the grave implications of not entering into this covenant, and the unforgivable act that God will not pardon.

Salvation to Those Who Believe

Why do we call the New Covenant a covenant of faith? Let's explore this idea.

Recall in chapter three, *Promise*, lesson three, *Promise of Faith*, that God had promised Abraham that one of his descendants would be the one to bless the nations. Abraham's faith foreshadows that the New Covenant is fundamentally about believing in God. This emphasis on faith is crucial to understanding the New Covenant. Keep this in mind as you continue in this study.

We can only be a party to the New Covenant and receive Jesus' righteousness if we put our faith in (believe in) Jesus. That not only means we believe He exists, but also that He did what He said He did to make us righteous. We must believe that His righteousness is good enough to pay the penalty for our sins and that by grace, He bestows His righteousness on us when we put our faith in Him. We must believe the gospel, or good news, and all that it contains.

It's important to note that we remain in the covenant by faith and faith alone. This means that our relationship with Jesus is not based on our ability to follow a set of commands, rules, or laws, but solely on our belief in Him and His grace. If we continue in that faith, and do not try to justify ourselves through our own works, we will remain in Him. We will investigate deeper into this concept as it relates to legalism in lesson three of this chapter, but in this lesson, we will focus on the essence of our faith in the New Covenant.

Let's take a brief look at scriptures that support our foundational truth.

Read *Acts 26:15-18*. In this section of Acts, Paul (who was called Saul at the time) is recounting his experience with the Lord when Jesus stopped him on the road to Damascus. At the end of verse 18, Jesus says that people would receive forgiveness of sins and an inheritance along with those who are sanctified by what?

Read *Romans 10:9*. If you believe in your heart, you will be what?

Read *Romans 10:10*. According to this verse, if you believe in your heart what do you receive?

And if you confess, what do you receive?

Read *Romans 10:11*. Paul quotes from Isaiah here. What benefit is there to those who believe?

Read *John 1:12-13*. How does John define those who believe in Jesus?

Read *John 11:25-26*. What does Jesus say one must do to never die?

Read *Acts 16:30-31*. These two verses plainly describe salvation. Simply believe.

Read *Romans 1:16-17*. This verse says that the righteousness of God is revealed from faith to faith. We come to Jesus by faith, and we live by what?

Read *2 Corinthians 5:7* How do we walk?

The Unpardonable Sin: Unbelief

If faith in Christ is the only thing that can save someone, then unbelief is the only thing that can condemn them.

Read *Hebrews 3:16-19*. The writer of Hebrews uses the people Moses led out of Egypt as an example for us about who will enter God's rest, or receive salvation. Why were they not allowed into the promised land according to verse 19?

Read *Colossians 1:21-23*. According to verse 23 what must you continue in?

And you must stay grounded, remain steadfast, and not move away from the hope of what?

Read *Romans 11:11-24*. Paul, speaking of the Israelites, makes the case that because of their unbelief they were cut off from the family of God, but that if we don't continue in the faith, we too might be cut off. He goes on to say that if they don't continue in unbelief, they will be grafted back in. If belief, then, is the deciding factor of salvation, then unbelief is the deciding factor of one's eternal death.

There is a fascinating passage in 1 John that speaks to this topic.

> Read *1 John 5:16*. How does John distinguish the two different types of sin he is talking about in this verse?

> Read the next verse, *1 John 5:17*. What do you think is the sin leading to death versus the sin not leading to death?

This idea may seem elementary, but I am making an essential point about your sin. I have heard so many Christ followers say they are afraid because they still sin to some degree. They fear that God might punish them, is not pleased with them, or they might not be welcomed into eternity. My friend, we can only separate ourselves from God through unbelief. You will be saved if you believe in Jesus and His righteousness for your own. The only unpardonable sin is to reject Jesus for your righteousness and refuse to believe in His grace.

The beautiful thing is, we can take this as truth, fully rest in our faith in the Son of God, and trust that He accepts us, loves us, and can't wait to receive us into His arms. Your sin cannot and does not invalidate your security of salvation by grace through faith in Jesus. It is so simple it is hard to fathom why people so often reject it. See *Chapter 10, The Separation Lie*, in *Radical Grace* for more on this topic.

Why Does it Matter to You?

Why do you think it matters that you know the New Covenant is a covenant of faith? What would it mean to you and your relationship with Jesus if it wasn't simply about belief, but also about your duty to fulfill certain laws, commands, or rules? How does this help to define God's radical grace?

Why it Matters to Grace

If our salvation, blessings, or relationship with Jesus is based on works, obedience, or anything other than faith, then His grace is made null. Our relationship with God is about our simple belief in His radical grace.

Confirm the Brick

Do you believe that the New Covenant is a covenant that is based solely on faith? You become a participant of the New Covenant by putting your faith in Jesus, and you remain in that covenant through your continued faith. If you agree, put a check next to the statement and never, ever, ever stop having faith.

The New Covenant offers salvation to those who believe.

The Covenant of Grace
Brick 15

"I marvel that you are turning away so soon from Him who called you in the grace of Christ, to a different gospel, which is not another; but there are some who trouble you and want to pervert the gospel of Christ."

Galatians 1:6-7

We are welcomed into the New Covenant by our faith in the righteousness of Jesus. Belief is all we need to become a member of the New Covenant. God's participation in the contract offers grace to all who believe. His grace drove Jesus to die for you and me to pay the penalty for our sins and cleanse us from all unrighteousness. His grace inspired Him to rise on the third day to offer us His righteousness, baptize us with the Holy Spirit, and make all things new. His grace now allows us to live in peace with God, to walk according to the Spirit, in love, and to rest in that grace. The New Covenant is a covenant of grace and does not require us to work for our salvation, righteousness, approval, holiness, forgiveness, acceptance, blessings, or any of the Father's promises.

The Foundational Truth

The New Covenant is one of grace, not works.

The New Covenant is a covenant of grace through faith. Grace and faith are counter to works. We have already learned that we are no longer under the Law but under grace. However, it seems that the Christian body struggles to live in the freedom that Jesus has afforded us through His death and resurrection. It's time we put all dead works to rest, both those dead works of the Law and those dead works that people say are necessary for godly Christian living. It is time to live in God's radical grace and walk by faith. Let's see what the Bible says about this topic.

Grace vs. Works

Legalism is what the Bible calls dead works. If we believe we can obtain righteousness through our good works of obedience to the Law or any manmade rules, those acts are called dead works, which are useless because Jesus already did the work for us. When we attempt to become righteous through our own works we are not receiving the grace of God by faith, and therefore, declaring Jesus' death and resurrection futile and worthless.

Recall ***Romans 4:1-4***. In verse four Paul tells us plainly that if we believe we are to work for our justification, also known as righteousness, the wages of that work would not be counted as God's grace, but as what?

God would owe us if we did certain things to obtain our righteousness. It doesn't work that way. We cannot earn our righteousness, which would make God indebted to us. God's gift of righteousness is given freely to those who have faith in His Son.

Paul's argument in the book of Romans, where he makes a clear distinction between grace and works, is a crucial one. He asserts that grace cannot be grace if it is by works, and vice versa. This concept, which we briefly discussed in chapter three, is worth revisiting in this context to further deepen our understanding.

Read ***Romans 11:6***. If it is by grace, it is no longer of what?

And if it is of works, it is no longer what?

Read ***Galatians 2:21***. Christ died in vain if righteousness comes through what?

If we cannot gain our righteousness through our works, it is useless that we are often encouraged to follow a list of dos and don'ts to become more holy or Christlike.

Continue in ***Colossians 2:11-15***. According to verse 14, what two things did Jesus do to the requirements that were against us?

Jesus took the Law and nailed it to His cross. So, what is Paul's point? Let's find out.

Read *Colossians 2:16*. Paul tells us not to let anyone judge us concerning what five things?

Read *Colossians 2:17*. Paul says these things are a shadow of what and what is the substance of these things?

Do not miss the power of what Paul is saying here. All those things that God required of the Jewish people to obey were not the real things. They were a shadow of the real thing, which is Jesus.

As we learned previously, the Law points us to Christ. Once we are in Christ, there is no need for the shadow; we get the real thing, Jesus, and His Spirit living in us.

Read *Colossians 2:18-19*. To what reward is Paul referring? Let's read more to find out.

Read *Colossians 2:20-22*. Paul asks why we subject ourselves to regulations. Paul tells us these regulations concern things which perish with their use.

Do these regulations come from God?   Yes   No

Who makes up these rules?

Read *Colossians 2:23*. According to this verse, these things look wise, but have no value against what?

What do you think is the reward Paul references in verse 18?

This verse amazes me. Paul tells us that no matter how hard we try to obey a list of rules and regulations, *"obedience"* in our flesh doesn't have any value toward eliminating our fleshly indulgences. In other words, striving to obey laws or rules doesn't help with our fleshly desires. Striving in the flesh to control our flesh doesn't work. Does that mean we are all sunk? Oh, no, my dear friend. God's radical grace is the answer. Let's continue.

Read *Romans 7:6*. We are now to serve not in the Law, but in the newness of who?

This is what makes the New Covenant so great!

Read *2 Corinthians 3:4-6*. The Spirit gives what?

In that new life, with the aid of the Helper, the Holy Spirit, we get to live, really live, as we walk in Him.

Read *2 Timothy 1:8-9*. Jesus saves us and calls us not according to what?

But according to what?

Grace means we don't have to work. Grace means we don't have a list of laws and regulations we must obey. Grace means we have liberty, not bondage.

Read *2 Corinthians 3:17*. Where the Spirit of the Lord is there is what?

Read *Galatians 2:4*. These men wanted to bring people back into the bondage that Jesus had released them from. What was it that they were spying out?

Sadly, though Jesus has set us free, some people try to bring us back into the bondage of legalistic obedience. If we firmly know that the New Covenant is a covenant of grace, then we will not be swayed or led astray into the legalistic practices of those who try to do so.

Finally, read *Galatians 1:6-7*. Paul marvels at how quickly the people of Galatia have allowed others to lead them away from Jesus. Paul tells us that those who are leading them away are using a perverted version of what?

The Galatians were being led astray into a false gospel of works.

C.O.D.E.

What is the C.O.D.E.? I created this acronym to define the legalistic measure of obedience versus disobedience to rules and laws that some Christians needlessly put on themselves. The acronym stands for **C**hristian **O**bedience-**D**isobedience **E**quation. You can look at it this way (like math):

(My obedient behaviors) – (My disobedient behaviors) = (My net obedience or disobedience.)

In other words, the things that I do good are weighed against the things that I do bad, and that difference or summary explains whether I can say I am obedient to God or not. The idea is that we hope the good outweighs the bad, and if that is so, we may consider ourselves obedient, good people, or more Christlike, and that we are pleasing God. This approach is steeped in legalism.

The C.O.D.E. defines the way many believers approach life. Because the Christian community often speaks about obedience, it grabs the attention of people who truly desire to make God happy, walk in righteousness, and be a faithful child of God. Those desires are good and noble. There is nothing wrong with wanting those things. However, we must realize that God doesn't require you to obey laws and rules to make Him happy, receive His righteousness, or be a faithful follower. Remember, your faith in Him is all He requires. God doesn't hold you responsible for completing a list of dos and don'ts created by people who are trapped in legalism and don't understand His grace.

When people talk about obedience, they often don't define it. The word just hangs out there like we are supposed to know exactly what it means, and for fear of seeming ignorant, we just go with it and act like we know what they are talking about. Meanwhile, we put our antennae up, hoping to hear what others say it means. We listen carefully to sermons, read books and articles, and check out social media, wishing someone would describe what it means to be obedient. We pick up and start to follow different rules and commands based on where we look and who we listen to.

When we are told to be obedient, we hear that we aren't righteous enough and must do better. Obedience to the Law or dead works isn't the path to righteousness; it is a placeholder for legalism.

So far in this chapter, we've learned that in the New Covenant, Jesus has done everything, and our part is to believe in this truth. The New Covenant is not about engaging in fruitless works, but about having faith. Yet, why do many allow the teachings of others to ensnare them in the cycle of works? I believe there are several reasons for this, which I will now discuss.

Reasons We Accept the C.O.D.E.

First, we are all engulfed in the worldly work-for-reward system: work hard, get rewarded, don't work, get punished. Therefore, it is difficult for some to realize and accept that God doesn't participate in that system.

It is a common teaching among the Christian community that we must do good deeds, stop doing bad things, and strive to be obedient to receive God's approval, blessings, and promises or to make Him happy. This teaching is what drives our adherence to the C.O.D.E. It seems we easily accept our duty to the C.O.D.E. because it is popular, instead of pausing to think about what the Bible says about works versus grace.

Grace means our relationship with Jesus isn't defined by *"have to."* Instead, it's defined by *"get to."* Grace says God loves us just the way we were, are, and will be, even though the world tells us daily that we aren't enough. Grace shouts from the rooftops that God baked in our value when He created us; our outward behavior does not determine it.

Second, a popular teaching states Christians must be obedient and do good works to prove or show they are saved. I'm sure you have heard someone say that we know who is a Christian because their fruits (meaning their behaviors or lifestyle) are the indicator. Others may judge us based on the things of this world, but grace says that God sees us and knows our hearts. Grace doesn't view us in the physical and material world; it views us in the spiritual and eternal kingdom. While judgment looks at what we do, grace sees our faith.

Third, some falsely believe that their sin separates them from God, so they need to be obedient to remain close to Jesus. Grace secures our relationship with God because satisfying the C.O.D.E. doesn't determine our bond with Him, but Jesus creates that bond through what He has already done. Grace says the work is finished and nothing can separate us from God's love. (See *Chapter 10* of *Radical Grace* for more on this subject.)

Lastly, some people believe God needs to work on them or discipline them for a time to make them ready to receive His promises. I do not deny that God does work with us to sharpen us, teach us new things, and inspire us to walk in love. He also allows the worldly consequences of our sin to affect us and those around us. Those consequences teach us and grow our understanding of the costs of walking in our flesh rather than in love and according to His Spirit. However, that process of learning and growing does not negate or delay our receiving of all the spiritual blessings and promises of God. In Christ, we are declared children of God, members of the heavenly kingdom, made righteous, cleansed, made holy, and receive the Holy Spirit as a guarantee of our trip into eternity. We receive those promises the moment we put our faith in Jesus' righteousness for our own. No completed list of works, walk through the desert for a time, or submission to the C.O.D.E. is required for us to receive those promised gifts. Grace doesn't rely on us to prepare for its arrival; it just shows up, and we may invite it into our lives.

Radical grace is like winning the lottery of the universe in which we receive all the good stuff of God. Wow! I can't help but praise God for His great gift of grace as I humbly admit I don't deserve it. Thank you, Jesus, for your radical grace!

Note

Please note that I understand that people who strive for obedience serve God the way they believe they should. They say they are obedient because of their love for God. Obedience isn't a bad word. Obedience means to trust someone and fully surrender to them. We can trust God and know that what He calls us to do is good for us and the world. I only take exception to this statement when obedience is a cloak for legalism. When people do things from the heart, those are not legalistic, dead works; they are works of righteousness as one walks in the Spirit. Obedience becomes legalism when one does a work in their flesh to try to earn something that God has already given them, to show God or others proof that they are saved, or because someone told them what they should be doing to be an obedient child of God. My heart is for everyone to understand God's grace as it is contrasted with the work of striving for obedience.

In chapter eight we will discuss the term *obedience* in the correct context of God's radical grace.

Why Does it Matter to You?

Why do you think it is important for you to understand that your relationship with Jesus is not about your good or bad behavior, but about His grace? If this is a new concept for you, how might this truth change your life?

Why it Matters to Grace

There is great comfort, joy, and peace in knowing that we are not subject to fulfilling a list of laws, rules, or regulations in the New Covenant. There are several reasons why it is important to know this is true.

First, you no longer waste your time striving against your sinful nature. Instead, you put your focus and time into living the new life Jesus gave you through your rebirth in the Spirit. That is radical grace.

Additionally, you may lay down any shame of inadequacy and rest knowing that God loves you just as you are, apart from your actions and behaviors. That is also radical grace.

Finally, rather than experiencing fear of acceptance and separation from God, you are secure in your faith and know that God is always with you. That is radical grace.

Confirm the Brick

Jesus initiated the New Covenant based on what He has done for you rather than what you can do in your own effort. You cannot make yourself righteous nor make God love you more through obedience to the Jewish Law or man's doctrines. If you believe this is true, confirm that this brick is a part of your understanding of the foundation of radical grace and put a check mark next to the statement below.

The New Covenant is one of grace, not works.

Build the Foundation of Radical Grace

It is time to cement these *New Covenant* bricks into your foundation of radical grace. Interestingly, the New Covenant *is* the good news of the Gospel. Having a thorough understanding of the New Covenant allows you to build an unshakable foundation of radical grace.

Bricks 13, 14, and 15: *New Covenant*

The facts:

God promised a new and better covenant.

The New Covenant is a covenant of faith.

The New Covenant is a covenant of grace.

Remember, once in place, you can't move or loosen these bricks.

Live Free and Unashamed

Remember when God rested on the seventh day after creating this beautiful universe? That rest symbolizes His grace, which allows us to rest in Jesus. Jesus said, *"For My yoke is easy and My burden is light"* (**Matthew 11:30**, NKJV). He also said, *"Come to Me, all you who labor and are heavy laden, and I will give you rest"* (**Matthew 11:28**, NKJV). Yes, these verses refer to our ultimate rest in eternity, but they also speak to our daily rest in the finished work of Christ. We may rest from our dead works because He ushered in the New Covenant of faith and grace (**Hebrews 9:14**).

Take these statements of His to heart. He is telling you that in Him, you don't have to work hard and carry a large load by yourself. In Christ, you don't have to repeatedly try and fail to fulfill the Mosaic Law or the C.O.D.E.

If you are heavy-laden or struggling to rest, I encourage you to find time to share your burdens with Jesus. Ask Him to show you what His grace means for your life. Grace will lighten your load. Take some time to meditate on the scriptures in this chapter. Jesus said He would give you rest. Believe Him.

For more in-depth information about this topic, read **Hebrews chapters 8, 9, and 10**.

Chapter 6

New You

"...that you put off, concerning your former conduct, the old man which grows corrupt according to the deceitful lusts, and be renewed in the spirit of your mind, and that you put on the new man which was created according to God, in true righteousness and holiness."

Ephesians 4:22-24

Duality is the characteristic of being or consisting of two parts. Understanding that we are a dual person in Christ is the most significant key to unlocking the truth that we are a new creation. The failure to understand our two natures in Christ has plagued Christianity since shortly after the disciples watched Jesus disappear into a cloud above them. This misunderstanding is the root of many legalistic tendencies in teachings we have seen since the time of the writing of the New Testament. The apostle Paul wrote extensively about this in his letters. He used the term "old man" to define our flesh and revealed that once we are born again, we are born of the Spirit as a "new man."

Now that we are a new creation in Christ, we must recognize that we have two separate natures but that our new spiritual part of us is our true identity. That new creation has been made righteous and holy. The old part of us that is our sinful nature still hangs around until we enter eternity, but the Word tells us we have died to it.

This concept of duality allows us to understand why we still fall short in our flesh, how the Father, who requires perfect righteousness, receives us anyway, and the beautiful gift He has provided us of being able to walk in our new nature, according to the Spirit. This knowledge keeps us from thinking that we need to work to make our old self more holy through legalistic works, which idea denies the radical grace of God.

In this chapter, we will learn about our new self who is both righteous and holy.

Read chapters 11-13 of *Radical Grace* if you are reading along with this study.

Born Again in Christ
Brick 16

"Jesus answered, 'Most assuredly, I say to you, unless one is born of water and the Spirit, he cannot enter the kingdom of God."

John 3:5

Have you ever pondered any of the following questions?

If I'm a new creation in Christ, why do I still sin?

If I am free from the bondage of sin, why do I still do it?

If I am made righteous, why do I still think unrighteous thoughts and do unrighteous things?

Let me tell you, my friend, if any of these questions are familiar, you are not alone. We all, as a community of believers, share these struggles. And because many people have failed to answer these questions in any meaningful way, many believers are left feeling confused, frustrated, and hopeless. Sadly, the resulting doctrines that attempt to make sense of the confusion lean toward legalism.

Teachers and preachers warn us that if we still sin, we are not holy enough; we need to control our behavior and work on becoming more holy. Though they say we aren't holy, that statement contradicts specific scriptures. The typical Christian message doesn't ever provide a real solution to this puzzle. We don't hear an explanation that is fully in line with all of Scripture and doesn't lead people away from the grace of God.

The good news, though, is that there is an answer that makes sense and doesn't contradict the Bible. Instead, it aligns and includes scriptures that seemingly contradict each other and otherwise don't make sense. The Bible teaches us that once we are born again, we have two natures; we have a new spiritually alive and clean nature, but we still have our flesh nature hanging around. That explains how we can be both holy and still drawn to sin at the same time.

Knowing and believing that we have two natures in Christ finally makes sense out of these seemingly contradictory ideas, frees us from the bondage of legalism, and aids in our understanding and receiving of God's radical grace.

In this lesson we examine what it means to be born again and the truth about the new you.

The Foundational Truth

In Christ, you have been born again and have two natures.

We will see that the Bible speaks of our duality in many ways. This concept of us having two natures is a significant aspect of the Gospel of Grace. Making us new is one of the main reasons why Jesus came to earth. He came to offer us to be born "again" into a spiritual existence, and once we are, He gives us His Spirit to reside inside us to help us walk in that new existence. We will learn that the concept of our dual natures clearly explains why we can identify as a new creation, be freed from sin, and be made righteous, yet still miss the mark more than we would hope.

The idea that you have two different natures may be a new concept for you, but once you fully grasp this concept, you will be amazed at how much this explains your experiences as a child of God. It will also free you from condemnation and help you on your quest to fully understand God's radical grace. This one concept is the catalyst that will rocket you toward living free and unashamed.

Born Again

I'm sure you have heard someone talk about being "born again." This two-word phrase became popular in the 1960s and 1970s and is often used to describe evangelical Christians. The nature of this phrase in English indicates that we are to be born a second time. And that is true in a sense. However, considering the Greek definition of *again*, it possesses a more powerful and beautiful message than being born twice. It indicates being *born from above*. (Blue Letter Bible, 2024) Being born again must be something extraordinary if it comes from above or from heaven, versus our first birth, which occurred below, on earth, in the physical realm. We are not just born a second time into our same circumstances; we are born anew from the spiritual heavenly realm. We are reborn spiritually from the heavenly kingdom. These two births indicate that we possess both a carnal or temporal and a spiritual or eternal existence.

For years, I had a simplistic understanding of what it meant to be born again; I knew it meant I was saved, but my understanding was vague at best. I knew the Bible said I was born again, but I had questions like those listed at the beginning of this chapter. If I had been made new, why did I still struggle with sin? See, I viewed myself as one *me*, and that *me* didn't seem very new after becoming a Christian. Upon learning that I was reborn by God spiritually from His heavenly realm, and that was the part of me that is made righteous and holy, the foggy confusion started to lift. That revelation helped me to see that I genuinely was made new. My struggle with sin was me just not knowing how to put off that old self and access my new spiritual nature.

Understanding being born again, or born from above, in the context of your duality should clear up any confusion you may have.

Let's start with the prophecy that God would give us a new spirit.

Read *Ezekiel 36:26-27*. The LORD God promises to give you a new heart and a new what?

Verse 27 says He will give you His Spirit, distinguishing His indwelling from your renewed spirit and softer heart.

We can see the distinction between our flesh and spirit if we simply look at the Word. In the book of John, Jesus spells it out plainly for us. Let's begin there.

Read *John 3:1-3*. What does Jesus say one must do to see the kingdom of God?

Read *John 3:4*. Nicodemus asked Jesus the question that we all would have asked. What did Nicodemus ask?

Read *John 3:5*. What are the two types of *birth* that Jesus mentions in His answer?

Read *John 3:6*. That which is born of the flesh, is what? And that of the Spirit, is what?

Read *John 3:7*. This is obviously an amazing and awe-inspiring concept as Jesus told Nicodemus not to do what at His statement?

Read *John 3:8*. What do you think Jesus meant by this verse?

Now, we know God requires us to be born again to enter the kingdom of God. We are born once in the flesh. Then, when we come to Jesus, we are born again in the spirit. Our two separate births create in us two separate natures. In chapter two of this study, we learned about our born-of-the-flesh person. Let's dig a little deeper into this born-of-the-spirit person.

The New You

In Christ, He gives us a newly remodeled spirit, which is a total game changer. Check out the Biblical evidence that we have a new nature.

Read **Romans 8:5-6**. To be carnally minded is what?

And to be spiritually minded is what?

According to these verses, where is it that we can distinguish whether we are living in our flesh or in our new spirit?

Why would being carnally minded be death?

And why would being spiritually minded be life and peace?

Read **Romans 8:7**. Who does Paul say our carnal mind is against?

Paul is saying our fleshly, carnal mind cannot even be subjected to the Law. Why do you suppose this is? (See the above questions and **Romans 8:2-3**. Note the two laws in verse 2.)

Read **Romans 8:8**. Can those who are in their flesh please God?   Yes   No

Good news! Read **Romans 8:9-11**. If the Spirit of God dwells in you, you are not in the flesh, but in what?

What does the Spirit give life to as He dwells in you according to verse 11?

See, our physical body is at the whim of our mindful choices. This verse shows us that the phrase, *in the flesh*, cannot refer to simply living in our physical bodies; rather, it refers to living in our sinful nature.

Read **Romans 8:12-14**. Who does verse 14 say the sons (and daughters) of God are led by?

If our flesh cannot please God, why do we strive in the flesh to do so? When we surrender to the Spirit and walk in Him rather than strive in the flesh, we do please God. We will explore more of what this looks like in the following few chapters.

Let's continue to explore our new selves.

Read **Romans 6:5-6**. What happened to our old self?

Therefore, we are no longer what?

Read **2 Corinthians 5:17**. What has passed away and become new?

This concept may be confusing. These verses say our old self has been crucified, so why is it that we still drag him or her around and do fleshly things? The crucifixion of our flesh is a spiritual matter. Obviously, our physical bodies have not been hung on a cross. However, our spiritual crucifixion creates a separation between our old flesh and our new spirit, and we are renewed in our minds so that we may choose to walk and live in our new nature rather than our old nature. Check out the following verses that speak to this renewal of our minds.

Read **Romans 12:2**. We can avoid being conformed to this fallen world by being transformed by the renewing of what?

Read *2 Corinthians 4:16-18*. Our outward man/woman is what?

But our inward man/woman is being what?

The things which are seen are what?

And the things which are unseen are what?

Read *Ephesians 4:20-24*. Notice the process here; put off that old self, **think differently**, then put on that new shiny you! Is this concept a new revelation for you?   Yes   No

We can finally understand our struggles if we understand that we now have a totally new spiritual nature alongside our old nature. We can see how we can be made new while also finding ourselves continuing to sin at times. Since we crucified our fleshly old self with Christ, we don't have to allow that sinful nature to control us because we can give that control to our new spiritual self. Sin doesn't hold our new nature in chains; our new self is in submission to and guidance of God's Spirit. Thanks to His Spirit living in us, we have that control and power. We can choose to walk according to His Spirit instead of in bondage to our fleshly nature. That's not an easy choice sometimes, but it is possible.

Read *Colossians 3:8-10*. What does Paul tell us to put off and put on?

This means *putting* is a choice.

Read *2 Peter 1:1-4*. Once we are in Christ, we receive the Spirit and, therefore, get to partake of His divine what?

Doesn't that passage in 2 Peter just make you want to leap up out or your seat and praise Jesus?

There is clear evidence in the Word that we have an old man or woman called our flesh or sinful nature. We were born into this carnal existence, but Jesus tells us that we must be born again, according to the Spirit, to be saved.

When we are born again from above, we receive the baptism of the Holy Spirit in our new nature. And when the Spirit baptizes us, we receive Him into our lives and enjoy His fellowship, guidance, and power. We are part flesh and part spiritual.

Great news! We will leave our fleshly sinful nature behind when we jet off to eternity.

Read *1 Corinthians 15:50-53*. Flesh and blood cannot inherit what?

Corruptible cannot inherit what?

Why Does it Matter to You?

Why do you think it is important to understand that you now have a *new you* that is born into God's righteousness by His Spirit through faith in Jesus? Does understanding this concept of duality strengthen your faith in Jesus and His radical grace?

Why it Matters to Grace

Do you see how knowing you have two natures frees you in God's grace? Jesus knows you still have your flesh, and He has grace with you. Likewise, when you miss the mark, you can also have grace for yourself. God desires us to walk according to the Spirit, but He knows we won't all the time. Doesn't that make what Jesus did for us amazing? He knows that our flesh is entirely selfish, prideful, and headstrong. Our sinful, fleshly nature makes it difficult for us, so Jesus came to give us a new way to live. He gave us a new nature to walk in and His Spirit to help us. Now, we can take control away from that old person who wants to get us into trouble and give that control to our new self, who is aligned with God. We can see His grace more clearly when we see this reality, and we can have more compassion and grace with ourselves, knowing that Jesus isn't condemning us for what He already paid for. He doesn't expect us to renovate our old man or woman; He wants us to live in the new one that He provided for us.

The concept of duality provides the justification for us not to judge others. If we understand that all of Christ's followers have an old self and a new self, we can see that we are all in the same boat. We all struggle with our flesh. No one is immune from it. At the same time, we are now spiritual beings. Jesus told the woman at the well that true worshippers will worship in spirit and truth (*John 4:23-24*). And Paul tells us that we no longer regard people according to their flesh (*2 Corinthians 5:16*). Our job is not to judge others by their flesh but to love who they are in their spirit.

Confirm the Brick

If you believe that you are a dual person who is both an old and a new creation at the same time, put a check mark next to the statement.

Yes, in Christ, I have been born again and have two natures.

Born Into Righteousness
Brick 17

*"For with the heart one believes unto righteousness,
and with the mouth confession is made unto salvation."*

Romans 10:10

In the previous lesson of this chapter, we discussed our old fleshly and renewed spiritual selves. The new part of us born again and created in Christ is declared righteous and made righteous. This concept may be news to you as many people teach that it is our job to work on becoming more righteous, or Christlike, through the effort to sin less and do more good works; in other words, be obedient. This teaching is a form of legalism and is in direct conflict with radical grace.

Recall that in chapter four, we learned that Jesus was the end of the Law for righteousness. In this lesson, we explore the scriptures that maintain that once you declare your faith in Jesus, He makes you righteous. Understanding that it is your new self that is righteous, not your old self helps to make sense of this concept.

The Foundational Truth

Through Jesus' death and resurrection, we are both declared righteous and made righteous.

Because sin still tempts us as followers of Christ, we have a hard time reconciling the Word when it says we are righteous. This problem stems from our need to understand that we have two different natures. Knowing our old self is separate from our new self helps us accept that it's not our old man or woman who is righteous but our newly reborn self. This concept explains that we can be righteous while still missing the mark at times.

Today's lesson is centered on a fundamental truth: the Bible unequivocally declares that we are righteous in Christ.

Justification

The word *justification* shows up quite a bit in the New Testament. We read words such as *justify*, *justified*, *justifier*, and *justification*. We must understand the definitions of these words to grasp the truth about righteousness.

Justification is the act of declaring someone righteous. So, when Jesus declares us righteous, innocent, and faultless through His act of redemption, we are justified. Jesus not only declares us innocent or righteous, but He also imputes His righteousness to us or puts His righteousness on our account. Jesus is the justifier, and when He makes us righteous, we are justified.

Let's look at the verses that state these truths.

Read ***Romans 3:21-22***. The righteousness of God is revealed apart from what and through what?

Read ***Romans 3:24***. Through redemption in Jesus we are what?

Read ***Romans 3:25-26***. Jesus is justifier of whom?

Jesus justifies those who have faith in Him by His grace and through His act of redemption. Let's look at more verses that speak to the fact that we are both declared righteous and credited with His righteousness.

Read ***Romans 5:15-19***. Through Adam's offense many will be condemned, but through Jesus, many will be made what?

Read ***Acts 13:38-39***. Paul tells us that no one can be justified by the Law, but by Jesus, everyone who believes is what?

Read ***Galatians 3:8*** and ***Romans 4:5-8***. Do you see the connection between our faith and the faith of Abraham?   Yes   No

Next read **Romans 4:13-25**. Notice the distinction between Jesus' death and His resurrection. According to verse 25, He had to die to pay the price for our offenses, and was raised for our what?

Read **Romans 10:10**. If we have a believing heart and confessing mouth, what do we receive?

Jesus, in His act of redemption, declares us righteous and graciously assigns His righteousness to us when we place our faith in Him. This act of divine grace is a constant source of reassurance and security in our faith.

In chapter two, *Righteousness*, I mentioned that we must meet God's standard of righteousness if we want to be with Him for eternity. Our attempt at becoming righteous will never achieve that standard. Additionally, when Jesus pays the price for our sins, His death doesn't make us righteous; it just means He paid our penalty, and our debt is forgiven. We still need to be made righteous to be with the Father in heaven. Therefore, Jesus also makes us righteous by imputing His righteousness to us. What a gift!

Training in Righteousness

Now that we are declared and made righteous, we need training. Jesus sent the Spirit to dwell in and help us, but we are babes learning to walk in this new nature. Note this interesting passage in 2 Timothy.

Read **2 Timothy 3:16**. This familiar passage contains an interesting phrase. We often focus on what Scripture is profitable *for*: doctrine, reproof, and correction. But what is Scripture profitable for instruction *in*?

Read **2 Timothy 3:17**. The Word instructs us in righteousness because now that we are righteous, we need to understand this new existence. For what purpose according to verse 17?

As we learn to walk in the new spiritual part of us, we will recognize when we are in our flesh versus when we are in the spirit. When we can distinguish between our two natures, we can walk in that righteous part of us as we submit to the Spirit instead of our sinful nature. We now have the power to choose to obey our flesh or obey our spirit. Look for more information about this in the following two chapters.

Read **Romans 6:12-14.** We can now present our whole body as instruments of what?

Verse 14 says that sin won't have dominion, or control of us because why?

Why Does it Matter to You?

Can you think of reasons why it would be beneficial for you to know and fully believe that you are, in fact, righteous? How does this truth impact your perspective of yourself and how you might approach your relationship with Jesus?

Why it Matters to Grace

What freedom we have in God's grace! We do not need to strive to become righteous through our efforts because Jesus has already done the work for us. Knowing that we are already righteous in our new spirit protects us from being drawn into a life of legalism and trying to fulfill the C.O.D.E. We may walk in righteousness and do righteous things because of God's radical grace.

Confirm the Brick

Do you believe that you are justified and have been made righteous? This means that you do not have to work at becoming more righteous through your efforts. If you agree with this brick, put a check by the following statement.

Yes, I have been both declared righteous and made righteous.

Born Into Holiness
Brick 18

"By that will we have been sanctified through the offering of the body of Jesus Christ once for all."

Hebrews 10:10

While many Bible teachers are comfortable declaring that those who are in Christ are righteous, there are still a number who have a difficult time stating that we are also holy. This difficulty may be because those teachers do not consider that they possess two natures. Without understanding our duality, it is impossible to reconcile.

There are verses in the Bible that state matter-of-factly that we *have been sanctified*. Shouldn't we take those verses seriously? In this lesson, I intend to do just that. We will carefully examine the evidence that we are considered holy as a child of God. We will also look at the myth of progressive sanctification so you may avoid being led into this false doctrine.

The Foundational Truth

We have been made holy through sanctification by the Spirit.

If you take a careful read of the New Testament you will find that the followers of Jesus are called holy and are declared sanctified. It is our newly created spiritual nature that is not only righteous, but it is also holy.

Sanctification

Sanctification means to be made holy. In Christ, we are sanctified in our renewed spiritual nature. Jesus makes us holy when we put our faith in Him and are made new. Today's lesson will investigate the overwhelming evidence that reveals this truth.

The confusion about sanctification hangs on the timing of our sanctification. Does the Word say we are *being* sanctified, or does it say we *have been* or *are* sanctified? Let's see what the Bible says.

Read **Acts 20:32**. We receive our inheritance among those who are what?

Read **Acts 26:15-18**. Let's note the dialogue between Paul and Jesus.

What does Jesus say people are sanctified by?

Does Jesus say people *will be* sanctified, or *are* sanctified?   Will be   Are

Note that sanctification is by faith. If we are made holy by faith, it is not by works or what we do. There is no progressive, self-determined process of sanctification.

Read **1 Corinthians 1:2**. Who is Paul addressing here?

Does Paul state that they are already sanctified?   Yes   No

Next read **1 Corinthians 6:9-11**. In verse 11, Paul tells the Corinthians they *were* what three things?

In whose name?

And by whom?

It looks like the Word is telling us that we have been sanctified, not that we will be sanctified later. However, there are a couple of verses that mention being sanctified. These are the verses on which the adherents to progressive sanctification base their doctrine. Let's look at them in context, to see what they say.

Read **Hebrews 2:10-11**.

I submit to you that the writer of Hebrews is talking about individuals who are being sanctified as they become members of the worldwide church. Notice that verse 10 says, *"...in bringing many sons to glory..."* The tense of the verb used here for *being sanctified* is present tense and means the action is occurring in actual time. This passage says that those who are coming into that glory, one by one, are being sanctified as they join the family, and it is a continual process as more and more "sons" come to glory. How can I assume this? Let's look a little further into Hebrews.

Read **Hebrews 10:8-10**. In verse 10, does the writer of Hebrews say we *are being* or *have been* sanctified?   Being   Have been

But wait, what about **Hebrews 10:14**? We are back to *being* sanctified. This verse is also speaking of those who are, in the present, coming to Christ, as if the reader was there watching it occur. Also notice the tense of "has perfected" in the verse. That sounds like a done deal.

Now read **Hebrews 10:28-29**. This passage warns us not to count Jesus' blood as a common thing and not to dismiss it as being insignificant. But look at who the writer is talking about doing the dismissing; it is he who was already sanctified by the blood of that covenant. The writer is talking about a follower of Christ who had already been sanctified.

Recall that if you are sanctified, that means you have been made holy. The following verses speak about being holy.

Read **1 Corinthians 7:14**. This verse is interesting. Because of a believing parent, their unbelieving spouse and their children are what?

Read **1 Corinthians 3:16-17**. You are the temple of God, and the temple of God is what?

Read **1 Peter 2:9**. You are what four things?

Read **Colossians 3:12**. As the elect of God, you are what and beloved?

Read **Hebrews 3:1**. The brethren are called what?

Lastly, revisit *Ephesians 4:24*. Our new man or woman was created according to God, in what two ways?

Our sanctification in Christ is not a distant concept, but a reality that we own. We are holy, as the Word affirms, and this truth liberates us from striving for holiness. More than that, we are empowered to live as the holy children of God that we are, engaging in spiritual works of righteousness.

Now, I know we don't always do that, do we? We will explore that more in the next chapter.

Progressive Sanctification

There is a common teaching within the Christian community that we must work on ourselves, with God's help, to become more holy or "Christlike." The technical term for this process is progressive sanctification. I believe the reason people follow this doctrine is because they cannot reconcile that if we are supposedly holy, we shouldn't continue to sin. I am mentioning this in this chapter about our new selves, as opposed to our old selves or our duality, because possessing two natures explains this problem. Our flesh is not and cannot be made holy. However, our spiritual nature that is born anew by the Spirit is sanctified and is, therefore, holy.

The most common scripture people use to defend the doctrine of progressive sanctification is *2 Corinthians 3:18*. I thoroughly examine this verse, and you can too, in chapter thirteen of *Radical Grace*, titled *The Sanctification Myth*. Still, I would also like to include a quick look at that verse in this study. We looked at this passage in an earlier chapter, but I'd like you to view it in the context of sanctification now.

Read *2 Corinthians 3:4-8*. Paul is comparing the Old and New Covenants. Verses 7 and 8 call each one the ministry of what?

Read *2 Corinthians 3:9*. This is a vital verse to note. Paul calls the Old Covenant a ministry of condemnation and the New Covenant a ministry of righteousness. The Old Covenant had glory, but the New Covenant exceeds much more in what?

Read *2 Corinthians 3:10-11*. What is much more glorious?

What remains refers to what?

Read *2 Corinthians 3:12-16*. Paul tells us that because of the exceeding glory of the New Covenant, he and his fellow ministers can speak boldly about the glorious New Covenant Gospel because when someone turns to the Lord, they are no longer blinded by the fading glory of the Old Covenant which is passing away.

Read *2 Corinthians 3:17*. Where the Spirit of the Lord is, there is what?

Why would Paul say this in the middle of this passage?

Now we get to the verse that causes people to stumble about sanctification.

Read *2 Corinthians 3:18*. With the background of this chapter of Corinthians in mind, and considering Paul's comparison of the glory of the Old Covenant to the exceeding glory of the New Covenant, who are the ones with an unveiled face?

What is reflected in the mirror?

The phrase, *beholding as in a mirror*, refers to what we see when we look into a mirror. The phrase, *are being transformed*, is the Greek word which is defined as *metamorphosis* in English. It means to be changed into another form. Again, it is in the present tense as if the reader is watching it occur.

What are "we" being transformed into?

The phrase, *from glory to glory*, is critical to understanding this verse. Many interpreters define the two glories as the glory of the person who is being transformed. They are suggesting that we have a little bit of glory, and our glory is being ratcheted up somehow over time. However, I believe we must look at context when interpreting Scripture.

What were the two things Paul was talking about that were glorious in verses 7 to 11?

Like the glory transformed from the Old Covenant to the much more glorious New Covenant through the Lord Jesus, we are transformed into the image of the Lord when we come to Him. Our face is unveiled, and we behold in the mirror our new spiritual self. It's like the mirror is a special spirit-nature mirror that reflects our new, reborn, and holy image.

Our transformation is not a gradual process, but an immediate change that occurs when we turn to the Lord, leaving the Old Covenant and its blinding veil behind. This verse in 2 Corinthians doesn't mention partnering with God to work on our sins or change our behavior to become holy. It tells us that we are transformed when we take off the veil of unbelief and put our faith in Christ as New Covenant believers. We are not progressively becoming holy. In Jesus, we **are holy**.

Why Does it Matter to You?

Can you think of any reasons why it would be beneficial for you to know and fully believe that you are, in fact, holy? How might this idea help you to walk in your new nature? How does this fact further define the God's radical grace?

Why it Matters to Grace

We do not have to take it upon ourselves to make ourselves holy. What a relief! I strove for over twenty years of my life trying to accomplish the impossible task of making my old self holy, not realizing that God had already done that work when I was born again, and He renewed my spirit. Grace means that through Jesus, our new man or woman is sanctified. We may lay down the burden of the legalistic works of progressive sanctification and truly rest in Jesus and His radical grace.

Confirm the Brick

Are you ready to confirm that this brick is truth? If you believe that, in Christ, you have been sanctified, put a check mark next to the statement, and enjoy your new life of freedom from having to strive to make yourself more holy.

Yes, I have been made holy by the Spirit.

Build the Foundation of Radical Grace

It is time to cement these *New You* bricks into your foundation of radical grace. Why do you need to place these bricks solidly into your foundation? This concept of being born again into a spiritual, righteous, and holy new nature while still having your old fleshly sinful nature is one of the few keys that explain some of the confusing doctrines you might hear, describes how you can be righteous and holy while still drawn into sin, and clarifies God's grace for you. You must cement this doctrine now because it will support what you will learn about in the coming chapters about your walk in Christ.

Bricks 16, 17, and 18: *New You*

The facts:

We are born again in Christ.

We are born into righteousness in Christ.

We are born into holiness in Christ.

Remember, once in place, you can't budge these bricks.

Live Free and Unashamed

Jesus came to give us a new identity, but we struggle to accept it. We humans often focus on the negatives. We think of ourselves from the perspective of our flaws, whether they are physical, mental, or spiritual. We rehearse how terrible we are based on our past mistakes. Negative self-talk fills our minds, and if we do succeed at anything, we get imposter syndrome and believe that we don't deserve success. It doesn't seem easy to even momentarily look at our accomplishments, good qualities, or compassionate concerns. We tell ourselves we can't pay attention to those positive things because that would be prideful. We Christians are supposed to be humble, but there is a fine line between humility and self-deprecation. While God calls us to be humble, godly humility encourages a realistic and honest assessment of ourselves. We shouldn't think too highly of our accomplishments, but at the same time, we don't need to underestimate our accomplishments either.

The Word tells you that God thoughtfully created you. You are unique, special, and beloved. Your failings are not who you are. Your old self is the pretender. The negative things you dwell on about yourself do not define you. Jesus came to set you free from that. He came to say that you are worth His time. You are worth His love. You are worth His life. He came to release you from that old, yucky person you think defines you and allow the beautiful person you are to shine forth and take center stage. That's the person that Jesus created. That's the person Jesus loves. That's the person to whom Jesus gave abundant and victorious life. All you need to do is recognize that wonderful person who is already righteous and holy and step into their shoes. That new you is truly who you are.

Chapter 7

Spirit

"The Spirit Himself bears witness with our spirit that we are children of God"

Romans 8:16

The Holy Spirit is such a blessing in our lives. I do not recall hearing much about Him during my early years going to church as a new believer. Because I didn't know much about Him, I thought He was only a means to do sensational things, such as speak in tongues or miraculously heal people. I had no idea His mission was far more relatable and personal to me than what I had heard.

Since those early days, I have learned much more about God and His Spirit. The New Testament explains some of what the Spirit does in this world and in the lives of those who put their faith in Christ. I have since learned that He is God who has come to live with us and lead us in this new life we have in Christ. He also draws us to Jesus and empowers us to walk in love.

In this chapter, we will first study who the Holy Spirit is, His mission for the world in general, and His mission for us. In lesson two, we will discuss what walking in the Spirit means. Lastly, we will talk about the concept of switching from walking in our flesh to walking in the Spirit, which I call the *Light switch*.

Read chapters 14-15 of *Radical Grace* if you are reading along with this study.

Pre-study Thoughts

What do you think is the Holy Spirit's mission in your life?

The Holy Spirit
Brick 19

"In Him you also trusted, after you heard the word of truth, the gospel of your salvation; in whom also, having believed, you were sealed with the Holy Spirit of promise..."

Ephesians 1:13

For many years, I didn't have a clue about the Holy Spirit. I knew He was a part of the Godhead, but I imagined Him as this mysterious presence that was distant and a bit scary. Boy, how wrong I was!

Because people don't understand the Spirit, they don't talk about Him much. Sadly, that lack of awareness and communication about Him causes people to miss what an amazing person (God) He is and how wonderful it is to be in fellowship with Him. Since I became a believer, I understood He lived in me, but I thought about that fact abstractly, not concretely. The Spirit is a person who lives inside of believers and communicates with our spirit. His mission is to help, give us strength, guide us, and provide us with everything we need to live our lives in Christ. What a beautiful and fantastic thing that the God and Creator of the universe would want to hang out with us 24/7!

The Foundational Truth

The Spirit of God lives in you, helps you, and guides you.

The Word of God reveals that when we are baptized with the Holy Spirit, He comes to dwell within us. His mission is deeply personal, empowering us to surrender our new spirit to His control, to love others, and to make spiritual decisions guided by His wisdom. For those who are not yet part of God's family, He has a different mission, but for us, He is always present, ready to comfort, guide, and even intercede for us with the Father.

We cannot know everything about the Spirit because He is God. However, we can learn a few things about Him through the Word. In this lesson, we will look at who the Holy Spirit is, what His mission is to the world, and what His mission is to us who have faith in Jesus.

The Spirit of God

Who is the Holy Spirit? The Bible gives us a fair amount of information about Him. Let's start with the basics of what we can glean from the Word.

He is the Spirit of God.

Read **Romans 8:9**. Paul refers to the Spirit as the Spirit of who, in this verse?

Read **1 Corinthians 3:16**. How is the Spirit referred to in this verse?

Read **John 4:24**. God is whom?

He is the third person of the trinity or triune, God.

Read **Matthew 28:19**. When speaking to the disciples, Jesus tells them to baptize people in the name of three people. Who are the three He is speaking about?

Read **1 John 5:7**. Recall from chapter one, who is the Word mentioned here?

The Father, the Word, and the Holy Spirit are what?

The Spirit's Mission

Jesus sent the Spirit of God on a mission. The Spirit's mission includes things He does for those in God's family and those not yet in God's family. Let's begin by looking at what His mission is to those who are not yet believers in Jesus.

Read *John 16:7-8*. What are the three things listed here that the Spirit will convict the world of?

Note that the *world* is distinguished from the believers. We can clearly see this distinction in the next verse.

Read *John 16:9*. He convicts the world of sin because of what reason?

The Spirit's mission is to show the world that they are sinful in hopes they look to Jesus for redemption.

Read *John 16:10-12*.

The Spirit's mission is to convince the world that the pursuit of righteousness through personal efforts will never work. Like believers, they need Jesus to make them righteous.

The Spirit's mission is also to reveal that judgment will come for those who follow Satan, the ruler of this world, instead of Jesus. Bringing people to Jesus is one of the main objectives of the Spirit.

Read *John 15:26*. What does John call the Spirit?

John refers to Him as the Spirit of what?

Who does the Spirit testify about?

Read *John 16:13-15*. What does this passage say the Spirit will do?

The Spirit will guide people into truth and glorify Jesus. Once we hear about Jesus and accept Him as our Savior, the Spirit is given to us. Let's look at that next.

Read *Mark 1:6-8*. Speaking about Jesus, John the baptizer says that Jesus will come and baptize us with whom?

Next reread *John 16:7*. Who sends the Spirit?

Jesus sends us His Spirit and baptizes us with Him.

What does it mean to be baptized by the Spirit?

Recall from chapter six that in *John 3:5,* Jesus said we must be born of water and the Spirit. Our first birth was by water (our physical birth) and our second birth was by the Spirit (our spiritual birth) when we put our faith in Jesus' righteousness for our own.

Note that one does not need to be baptized by water to receive the baptism of the Spirit. We see this in practice in *Acts 10:44-48*. The Gentiles were baptized by the Spirit and then were offered a water baptism. Furthermore, one can hear the Gospel but not yet receive the Spirit. We see this situation in *Acts 8:14-17*. The Samaritans heard the Gospel and received a water baptism, but the Spirit hadn't baptized them. The Bible doesn't explain why the Samaritans hadn't received the Spirit even though they believed the Gospel. There are as many opinions about this topic as there are denominations. It is not worth arguing about. However, the fact remains, we receive the Holy Spirit when we put our faith in Christ. I do not know the specific timing of receiving the Spirit for anyone. I leave that information in the hands of God.

Additionally, some people distinguish between being baptized with the Spirit and being filled with the Spirit. Again, I have my opinion on the subject, but I can't claim that I know the absolute truth, so I won't. The point is, however, that Jesus promised to send the Spirit as a guarantee of our salvation.

\Read *Acts 2:36-39*. Peter spoke to the people in Jerusalem about Jesus. They asked Peter and the disciples what they must do.

Peter's answer was what?

And what gift did he say they would receive?

Read *John 14:16-17*. Jesus says the Spirit will be with us, and where?

115

Read *Romans 8:9-11*. Again, where does the Spirit dwell?

We see then that Jesus sends us the Spirit to help us. Now, let's look at some of the blessings of His mission.

Read *2 Corinthians 1:21-22* and *5:5*. The Spirit is in our hearts as a what?

Read *Ephesians 1:13-14*. A guarantee of what?

Read *1 Corinthians 6:11*. What three things did the Spirit do for you?

Read *John 14:26*. What will the Spirit teach you?

Read *Romans 8:26-27*. What does the Spirit do for us?

Read *1 Corinthians 12:4-11*. What does the Spirit distribute to each one of us?

Read *Acts 9:31*. What does the Spirit do for us according to this verse?

Read *Romans 8:14* and *Galatians 5:18*. Who do these verses mention as the one who leads us?

Read *Galatians 5:22-23*. The Spirit produces fruit in our lives. Make a list of that fruit.

Read *Acts 2:4*. The Spirit may give us the ability to do what?

God sent His Spirit into the world to draw people to Jesus so they might be saved. Once saved, we are baptized with His Spirit, who lives in us, helping, guiding, and comforting us daily. He gives us spiritual gifts we use to bless others and work in His kingdom, and He produces fruit in us that we may share with the world around us. I like to think of the Spirit as my counselor, whom I have free access to 24/7 and who guides me toward peace, reconciliation, forgiveness, and love for others.

Why Does it Matter to You?

Why might it be important for you to understand who the Holy Spirit is and how might that affect your everyday walk in Christ?

Why it Matters to Grace

God, the Creator of the universe, has come to live amongst His children. What an amazing God who would come and reside within us, helping us every day to walk in love. Not only did Jesus redeem us from our inevitable condemnation, but He sent a Helper to assist us with this life. We receive Him because of His grace, and because we receive Him, we may have grace with others as He pours out His love into our hearts. The Spirit is the guarantee of God's grace as well as the power for us to share grace with others. Without the Spirit, our mission would be hopeless, as we would not be able to love the way God asks us to love. That is radical.

Confirm the Brick

Do you agree that the Spirit is God, He dwells in you, and His mission is to help and guide you in many ways? If so, put a check mark by the following statement.

Yes, the Spirit of God lives in me, helps me, and guides me.

Walk in the Spirit
Brick 20

"If we live in the Spirit, let us also walk in the Spirit."

Galatians 5:25

Now that the Spirit is living in us and our spirit is renewed, we have the best possible situation to build spiritual habits. By God's radical grace, we have a miraculous gift! If we have this gift of the Spirit living in us, let us also partake of His presence!

The Foundational Truth

Jesus gave us the Holy Spirit and we can walk in Him.

This concept of walking in the Spirit is prevalent in the Word yet is not often spoken of in the Christian community. Because many misunderstand walking in the Spirit, we often avoid the topic without realizing the benefit of the gift of the indwelling of the Spirit. As our lesson scripture says, if we have the Spirit living in us, let us also walk in Him.

Today's lesson is a practical exploration of the gifts bestowed upon us by the Holy Spirit; gifts that we can use as we walk in Him. We'll also examine scriptures that provide a clear picture of what it means to walk in the Spirit. Understanding this concept will enable us to discern whether we're operating in our flesh or in our spirit at any given moment and will inspire us to let the Spirit guide our lives.

The Spirit's Gifts

Now that we have the Spirit living in us, He provides many gifts for us to use for His kingdom. We have already discussed that God makes us righteous and holy, forgives our sins, and doesn't remember them anymore. These are tremendous examples of God's radical grace. But there are more gifts than these, and we will discuss some of them now.

Read **1 Corinthians 12:7-11**. List the gifts mentioned in this passage.

This list shows us some things we can do while walking in the Spirit. We might offer a word of wisdom to someone seeking answers or interpret what God said through someone as they spoke in tongues.

The Spirit also produces fruit in us. Recall the list you made in lesson one of this chapter.

Remember, it is the Spirit who is the true source of the fruit. We cannot produce these virtues. It is God who creates the fruit. We can only utilize them, and it is the Spirit who brings them to life within us. This understanding is crucial to prevent us from wasting our time thinking we need to pray to receive them or muster them up in our flesh when they are always available to us in our spirit. Knowing that these virtues are always available to us, we can tap into this divine reserve when needed and share these fruits with others.

As children of God, we have a renewed spiritual self, God's Spirit with us, His fruit to hand out, and the freedom to walk in Him. Jesus has given us everything we need. It's time to walk! What does that walk look like? Let's see some examples to help us know.

Snapshots of Walking in the Spirit

When the Bible talks about walking in the Spirit, it means living our daily lives in Him and submitting to His lead. It means to walk in our spirit, not our flesh. But how do we know the difference between walking in the Spirit versus walking in our flesh? Let's find out by looking at a section of Romans chapter twelve. These exhortations are a picture of walking in the Spirit.

Read **Romans 12:9**. Love should be without what?

Read **Romans 12:10**. Summarize this snapshot.

Read **Romans 12:11**. What three things are listed?

Read *Romans 12:12*. What does this verse say spiritual walking looks like?

Read *Romans 12:13*. How can we serve others in the Spirit according to this verse?

Read *Romans 12:14*. What fruits of the Spirit are related to this exhortation?

Read *Romans 12:15*. What word would you use to define this encouragement?

Read *Romans 12:16*. Summarize this snapshot.

Read *Romans 12:17*. Does this verse remind you of any other verse in the Word? If so, which verse?

Read *Romans 12:18*. What do you think about the fact that it says, *...if it is possible*?

Read *Romans 12:19-20*. How does walking in the Spirit look according to these verses?

Read *Romans 12:21*. This last verse summarizes being led by the Spirit in what way?

Read *2 Peter 1:1-4*. What are we partakers of?

This is just one section of the Bible that gives us a snapshot of what walking in the Spirit might look like. As you read your Bible, note any verses that give you a snapshot of walking in your spirit by the power of the Holy Spirit.

I must mention that these are not "The Commandments of Paul," as I've heard them called, for our commandments come from God and God alone. Nor are they a New Covenant list of commandments that we must strive to check off our to-do list. I referred to these as snapshots because they are our inspiration for what it looks like to walk in the Spirit and encouragements to walk in love.

I have found the fruit of the Spirit to be a helpful guide for me to know when I am in my flesh. I know that if I am inhabiting the opposite of the fruit of the Spirit, I am in my flesh. We can determine if we are being led by the Spirit or our flesh if we are being...

Loving or Hateful

Joyous or Miserable

Peaceful or Hostile

Patient or Short Tempered / Intolerant

Kind or Mean

Good or Wicked / Evil

Faithful or Disloyal / Unreliable

Gentle or Brutal

Self-Controlled or Unconstrained

Again, the list on the left should not be placed on your fridge, so you can check each off weekly. It isn't a prayer request to make your flesh better, either. Don't approach this list as a legalistic to-do list that you must strive to accomplish to make God happy. It is simply a mirror for you to look at your current mindset and behavior to ascertain whether you are in your flesh or your spirit. It is a great tool to reveal your state of mind and to guide you into walking in the Spirit. It is also a list of inspirational goals for walking in the Spirit.

Take stock of your walk with God as you move through life. You don't have to do something crazy amazing like heal someone, speak in tongues, or prophecy to be doing godly things. You can affect the world around you in tremendous ways through the million little things you do daily. Think about the list of fruits and how you already walk in them. When you are kind to your neighbor, soak in the joy of watching your kids play, or are patient with your grandparents, you are walking according to the Spirit. Those are miraculous moments. Those moments are made possible by God's love that He poured into your new heart. He has already given you all the tools you need to walk in the Spirit.

There is one more verse I'd like you to read.

Read *Galatians 5:16*. When we are walking in the Spirit, can our flesh be fulfilled?   Yes   No

This verse in Galatians was transformational for me. When I saw it from the perspective of walking in the spirit versus walking in the flesh, I realized that when we choose to give control to our spirit, our flesh cannot be in control. We can't do both at the same time. If we are "on" in our spirit, we are "off" in our flesh, and vice versa. This idea is tremendously helpful to understand as we seek to walk in righteousness.

Within the Christian community, there is far too much attention and emphasis placed on our sin. We have normalized focusing on our flesh and its failures. We talk about it, think about it, sing about it, and preach about it as if we can clean up our old man or woman. Let's normalize talking about, paying attention to, and emphasizing our walk in the Spirit instead and see what God will do with that. We will look at this concept further in the next lesson.

Why Does it Matter to You?

Why do you suppose it matters whether you seek to walk in the Spirit or not? How does walking or not walking in Him affect your daily life?

Why it Matters to Grace

Walking in the Spirit represents grace in two ways. First, we can do so because of God's grace. Jesus justified and sanctified us so that He could send His Spirit to come and live in us even though we were unrighteous sinners. That is radical grace. Second, as we walk in the Spirit, we will be handing out His fruit to the world around us, which is what giving grace to others looks like. That is how walking in love is defined. God knew we couldn't love others the way He intended unless, by His grace, He gave us the ability, motive, and power through His own Spirit to do so.

Confirm the Brick

Are you ready confirm that you believe you not only have the Spirit living in you, but that you also may live and walk in Him daily? If so, put a check mark by the following statement.

Yes, I have been given the Holy Spirit and I can walk in Him.

The Light Switch
Brick 21

"But put on the Lord Jesus Christ, and make no provision for the flesh, to fulfill its lusts."

Romans 13:14

In lesson two of this chapter, we saw snapshots of what walking in the Spirit can look like. But how do we do that? Our flesh is pretty determined to undermine us, drag us down, and keep us from serving and loving others. How do we switch from our flesh to our spirit, especially when hunkered down deep in our anger, selfishness, or pride?

At the beginning of chapter fifteen of *Radical Grace*, I give a hypothetical scenario that describes a common situation people have experienced. Here is what I wrote:

"You are arguing with someone. Ugly words are being exchanged and your blood is boiling. Then, the phone rings. You can't ignore this call, but you can't reveal to the caller you're in the middle of a heated discussion. What do you do? You switch your attitude immediately and answer in a kind, normal voice, 'Hello?'" (Appel, 2022, p. 124)

We all have had those times when we are in our flesh, and someone or something happens that makes us snap out of it and immediately act as if nothing is wrong. I call that situation flipping our Light switch. I capitalized Light because Jesus is the Light of the world (***John 1:6-7***), and Jesus also calls us the light of the world (***Matthew 5:14***). When we let our light shine, our good works glorify God (***Matthew 5:16***).

We are all familiar with that situation or something similar, but how do we consciously make that switch? Today's lesson will help you with the answer to that question.

The Foundational Truth

We have the choice to walk in our flesh or to walk in our spirit.

Because we have the Holy Spirit living in us, we have His strength to help us flip on our Light switch and walk in our spirit nature rather than our flesh. We can put off our ugly old self and put on our new righteous self in a flash, and that makes walking in the Spirit accessible any time.

The writers of the Bible offer many exhortations to walk in righteousness, in love, and according to the Spirit. Our lesson verse from Romans speaks about putting on Jesus. Paul's urging us to do so is critical to understanding how to submit ourselves to the leadership of the Spirit.

In this lesson, we look at the three basic steps to flipping the Light switch and walking in the Spirit.

Step 1: Knowing You Can

The first step to doing anything is knowing that it is possible. The Word mentions that we should walk in our new life. If we *should*, that means we *can*.

Read ***Romans 6:4-13***. This passage tells us that we *can* present our members as instruments of what?

Read ***Romans 8:9-11***. Life is given to our mortal bodies through whom?

Read ***Romans 8:12-14***. Verse 12 says we don't have to live according to what?

What happens if you live by the Spirit?

Who are the sons (and daughters) of God?

The Word tells us that we can be led by the Spirit, which means we may choose to walk in Him.

Step 2: Desiring to Walk in the Spirit

If you follow Jesus, I'm guessing that even though you don't always, you desire to walk in righteousness and according to the Spirit. None of us like hurting others or dealing with the consequences of our fleshly actions, but we also know that our flesh is a monster and demands to be in control. The second step to walking in the Spirit is desiring to walk according to the Spirit.

Read *Philippians 2:13*. Who is it that works in you to desire and do things that please Him?

Because we have the Spirit living in us, our new spirit desires to walk in Him. We hope for the time when we can leave this fleshly old self behind and stop fighting him or her for control. But until that happens, while we still live on this planet, God gave us a way to circumvent that old demanding flesh and walk in the Spirit. Now that we know it's possible and we have a desire to do so, we will look at the process of flipping the switch from our flesh to our spirit.

Step 3: Choosing to Flip Your Switch

Like the example I gave previously from *Radical Grace*, we can choose to flip that switch at any time. You've done it before; you just need to recognize that that is what you did. If you have ever immediately jumped from doing something in your flesh like yelling, gossiping, or being heatedly angry, to the opposite, like being calm, cool, and collected, to save embarrassment or avoid shame, you flipped on your Light switch. It really is just a choice, not an easy one sometimes, but it is a choice that is possible.

Read *Ephesians 4:17-18*. The Gentiles walk in the futility of what?

What does that mean?

Read *Ephesians 4:19*. This verse says the Gentiles have given themselves over to what?

Notice it says they *have given themselves* over to these things. This represents a choice.

Read *Ephesians 4:20-22*. What choice is presented in these verses?

Read *Ephesians 4:23*. Where are you renewed?

Read *Ephesians 4:24*. What choice is presented in this verse?

Read *Ephesians 4:25-32*. Do you see the pattern of the choices we can make?   Yes   No

These choices are always available to us. We just need to realize that we can make the choices that we desire in our spirit. It is a matter of choosing our spirit instead of allowing our flesh to win. Our flesh is determined, but that doesn't mean we can't switch it off and allow our spirit to have control. When we struggle, we should remember that we have the Spirit's power to help us.

One of the reasons I struggled to let go of my flesh was that I wasn't putting my total trust in Jesus. I was worried that if I didn't retain control of a situation, such as an argument, the other person wouldn't get my point, wouldn't change, wouldn't fix their behavior, wouldn't apologize, and wouldn't treat me better in the future. Isn't this often why we hang on to our anger toward others?

I believe that trusting God is the answer to how we give control to our spirit, which in turn hands that control to God's Spirit. And the Holy Spirit provides us the power to do so.

Read *Romans 8:28*. How do all things work for those who love God?

Read *2 Corinthians 5:7*. We walk by what?

Trusting God is the definition of walking by faith. God has our backs.

Read *Colossians 3:12-14*. Above all else, put on what?

The Bible encourages us to put off our old self and put on our new self. The fact is, we can make this switch at any time. It is common for people to think that because of their sin, they cannot make this switch. They see themselves in their fallen state and feel ashamed.

Nothing is holding us back from walking in righteousness. Whatever we just did in the flesh doesn't hinder us from walking in the Spirit in the next moment. Turn back to the Light immediately. We can flip our switch, independent of its position a second ago.

It has been beneficial for me to identify the triggers that stimulate my flesh. You can do this too. Be aware of those triggers and be prepared to respond to temptations rather than react in your flesh. Pray for the Spirit to assist you and give you the strength to handle difficult situations and to love people. Put off your old self, change your thinking, and put on your new self. Normalize walking in the Spirit.

This decision to walk according to the Spirit rather than the flesh is not an easy one sometimes. It seems impossible when you think about it. But I want to encourage you that you are capable of more than you think when you have God in your corner.

I know that different people struggle with their flesh to varying degrees. Some don't struggle much, while others have a hard time with anger or might battle their flesh over insecurity or depression. I want to encourage you that if you are in the trenches daily, at war with your flesh, first, take heart that that ugly flesh is not who you are in Jesus; it is not your true identity. And second, you might want to get some help with the things overwhelming you. I did; you can, too. You are worth it.

For more information about practicing switching to the Light, check out chapter fifteen of *Radical Grace*, titled *The Light Switch*. In that chapter, I provide several real-life examples of how this process works.

Why Does it Matter to You?

Knowing that you *can* walk in your spirit in submission to God's Spirit at any moment and in any situation, how might that affect your life, relationships, and wellbeing if you choose not to give in to your flesh, but choose to walk in love instead?

Why it Matters to Grace

God's radical grace has provided us with everything we need to walk in love. Jesus released us from the bondage of our sin, He made us holy and righteous, and then He sent His Spirit to come live in us. Now that we have all the tools and capabilities to walk in the Spirit, we can choose to flip on our Light switch. God's grace has allowed us to walk in love, and the implications of that ability run far and wide. When we normalize walking in the Spirit, our lives improve in many ways, from our relationships to our mental health.

Confirm the Brick

Put a check mark beside the statement if you agree that because you have dual natures, you may choose to walk in either your flesh or your spirit at any time. Having the choice doesn't mean it is easy, but you have the choice, nonetheless.

Yes, I can choose to switch from walking in my flesh to walking in my spirit.

Build the Foundation of Radical Grace

It is time to cement these Spirit bricks into your foundation of radical grace. The Spirit is such a blessed gift! Once you place this brick firmly into your foundation, you will see amazing changes in your life. You don't have to hang on to anger. You don't have to fear outcomes. You don't have to submit to your flesh's desires. The Spirit of God is there to help you flip on your Light.

Bricks 19, 20, and 21: *Spirit*

The facts:

Jesus sent the Holy Spirit to earth to baptize you into the spiritual kingdom of God and to live inside you, offering you His power and help.

We can walk in the Spirit.

We can flip from our flesh to our spirit like flipping a light switch.

Remember, once in place, these bricks can't be moved.

Live Free and Unashamed

When we think about our spiritual walk, we focus far too much on our failures and sins. Sure, we fail sometimes, and this world ensures we know it. People point out our bad behavior all the time. It gets a little old, doesn't it? And depressing. But what if we try to change that, at least when and where we have that choice? What might that do for those who cross our paths? What if we start celebrating Jesus and what He has done in us and others instead of zeroing in on what He already paid for?

The whole purpose of walking according to the Spirit is to love others and to have grace with them. An encouraging word can set someone on a path they never dreamed possible. A helping hand can lift a person's spirit and make them feel loved. But perhaps the most powerful act is forgiving an offender, as it opens the door for them to see the face of God which might change the direction of their eternal destiny. And a simple smile can offer hope to someone who is lost in despair. Love and grace, when practiced, are more powerful than any reminder of our failures, inspiring transformation, hope, and peace.

Chapter 8

Love

"And now abide faith, hope, love, these three; but the greatest of these is love."

1 Corinthians 13:13

In chapter five, *New Covenant*, I said, *"Obedience to the Law or dead works isn't the path to righteousness; it is a placeholder for legalism."*

I also said, *"...when people talk about obedience, they often don't define it. The word just hangs out there like we are supposed to know exactly what it means, and for fear of seeming ignorant, we just go with it and act like we know what they are talking about."*

As followers of Christ, we inherently know that obeying God is a good thing; of course, it is what He wants from us. Accordingly, when we hear someone tell us to be obedient, we nod in agreement and try to ignore the feeling of shame as we recall our undoubtedly disobedient behaviors of the week. The neglect of a clear definition of New Covenant obedience produces that shame. Obedience is not wrong, but it becomes legalistic when obedience leads us away from God's amazing radical grace and into a life of fleshly works. Rather than falling into the trap of obedience by fleshly works of the Old Covenant, we can walk in spiritual obedience to God as New Covenant believers.

So, what is New Covenant spiritual obedience? In this chapter, we look at the true definition of obedience which is according to the Word. Obedience is spiritual, not fleshly, and when we obey from within our renewed nature, our outer actions align with our inner spirit. We will see that obedience is not about following laws, rules, or regulations, but it is about grace. It is not about legalism; it is about freedom. And it is not about dead works, it is about life-giving love, liberating us from the burden of legalism.

Read chapter 16 of *Radical Grace* if you are reading along with this study.

The Commandments of Jesus
Brick 22

"You are My friends if you do whatever I command you."

John 15:14

In previous chapters, we learned that we are no longer under the Law of Moses and are not required to fulfill it because Jesus did that for us. We also learned that striving to obey the Law or the Ten Commandments will not make us righteous and can lead to a legalistic approach to obedience. Though we are not required to obey the Old Covenant commands, there are New Covenant commands that we are to follow. Jesus gave us two commands, which are what we will explore in this lesson.

The difference between New Covenant spiritual obedience and obedience as a work of the flesh is what this lesson is about. Faithful obedience in Christ is not a legalistic dog whistle for you to strive for obedience in the flesh. True obedience is about loving God and others. Love is the definition of walking in the Spirit.

The Foundational Truth

Jesus' new commandments are to love God and to love one another.

Jesus tells us plainly that He is giving us a new commandment to love. He fulfilled the old commandments, so we don't have to. In fact, loving Him and loving our neighbor has always been the goal. Humanity has failed miserably at accomplishing the goal of love, so Jesus came to fix that through fulfilling the Law, His death and resurrection, making us righteous, and sending us the Holy Spirit to live in us. He gave us everything we needed to succeed in loving one another. Jesus freed us from the works of the Law so that we could walk according to the Spirit, in love, and by His radical grace.

Law of Love

People commonly use the same verse to say we must obey the Mosaic Old Covenant Law. Let's see what that verse is about. Knowing the context of the verse will keep you from being led astray about it and from a legalistic approach to obedience.

Read *John 14:15*. This verse records Jesus saying that if you love Him, what?

Could Jesus be talking about the commandments from the Old Covenant? Technically, the Old Covenant was still in place when Jesus spoke these words because He hadn't died and risen again. However, as we have learned, in the New Covenant, Jesus fulfilled the Law. Therefore, it is not our goal to fulfill it. That means Jesus must have meant something different than keeping the Law of Moses if He was speaking to His future followers like you and me. Let's dig into this a bit.

In Matthew, we read about one of the Pharisees who attempted to test Jesus by asking Him, *"Teacher, which is the great commandment in the Law?"* (*Matthew 22:36*, NKJV). Let's look at Jesus' answer.

Read *Matthew 22:37-39*. What are the two commandments that Jesus defined as the two greatest commandments?

Jesus quoted from Deuteronomy 6:5 and Leviticus 19:18.

Read *Matthew 22:40*. What does the entire Old Testament hang from?

What is the important word in both commandments Jesus gave?

Read *1 John 2:3-7*. What old commandment does John refer to?

Read *1 John 2:8-10*. What commandment does John call new?

Read *John 13:33-35*. Jesus specifically said this is a new commandment. What is that commandment?

Read *John 15:9-17*. In verse 10 we see that Jesus distinguished His commandments from His Father's commandments. He stated that He kept His Father's commandments. What commandments was Jesus referring to?

Jesus spoke clearly in verse 12 when He said, *"This is my commandment..."* What is that commandment?

Read *Romans 13:8-10* and *Galatians 5:14*. According to Paul what is it that love fulfills?

Do you see that love is the fulfillment of and summation of the old commandments or Law? Love is also the one thing we must cherish as New Covenant believers. Jesus told us that we are to love God and love one another. He also gave us the Holy Spirit so we could do just that. We already read John 14:15 but note what Jesus said.

Read *John 14:15-18*. Right after Jesus said to keep His commandments, what did He say He will give us?

Jesus will not leave us as what?

Jesus promised to send us the Spirit, a powerful force that guides us in our journey. One of the Spirit's remarkable abilities is to help us walk in love. It's through the Spirit's power that we can love others. When love is a spiritual act, not a work of the flesh, it creates life, reconciliation, joy, peace, forgiveness, and grace. This is the radical nature of Godly love.

If anyone uses John 14:15 to try to lead you into obeying the Mosaic Law or guilt you for not making the fulfillment of the Mosaic Law your goal, do not allow it. You know the truth. Jesus wants you to keep His commands, but those commands are simply to love God and others. You are a New Covenant believer under grace; you are not under the Law of the Old Covenant.

Why Does it Matter to You?

Why is it important for you to know what commandments Jesus gave us as New Covenant believers? Considering what you have learned in this study, why can't you just follow the Ten Commandments? How does the Spirit play a part of your fulfilling of Jesus' new commands?

Why it Matters to Grace

We have learned that striving to fulfill the Law is the opposite of God's grace. If we believe that our duty is to fulfill the Law of Moses, we are striving in the flesh to be righteous and calling Jesus' death vain (*Galatians 2:21*). Any effort we put forth toward becoming righteous in our flesh is in direct competition with Jesus and what He has already done for us. We are freed from struggling to fulfill the Old Covenant Law and from approaching our relationship with Christ in a legalistic manner. We are free from legalism, and we know that loving God and loving one another are the only commandments we are to keep. That makes our mission in Christ straightforward, and it drives us to walk in the Spirit rather than strive in the flesh, which keeps us from a legalistic approach to love.

Confirm the Brick

Jesus summarized the old Law into two commandments for us. These two commandments describe the heart of God and what He has always desired from us. Being obedient in the New Covenant means to love. If you believe this is truth, place a check mark next to the statement below.

Yes, Jesus' new commandments are to love God and to love one another.

Love God

Brick 23

"Whoever believes that Jesus is the Christ is born of God, and everyone who loves Him who begot also loves him who is begotten of Him."

1 John 5:1

If you search online for *obedience in the Christian faith*, you will find a nauseating long list of legalistic articles. The problem is that most people's definition of obedience focuses on a change in our behavior through following orders, rules, laws, and Christian to-do lists (the C.O.D.E.), all actions in our flesh. Recall from chapter six, *New You*, that in our flesh nothing good dwells; it grows corrupt, is weak, profits us nothing, lusts against our spirit, and we should have no confidence in it. If we try to be obedient in our flesh by striving to change our outward behavior, we might succeed for a time, but inevitably, we will fail, and our flesh will win. The definition of *obedience* as *a change in what you do and say* misses the root of the change and transformation that believers receive from the Lord.

Biblical obedience isn't accomplished by modifying our behaviors in our flesh to become more holy or righteous but by understanding that the Spirit has already changed us because of our faith in Jesus. With our renewed heart, soul, and mind, we now operate with new spiritual and loving motivation, which will drive our behavior. And all of this is because we love God. What we say and do will be born out of our new heart of love.

In lesson one, *The Commandments of Jesus*, we read that Jesus said the first and greatest commandment is to love God and that if we love Him, we will keep His commandments. To obey God is to love Him and to love Him is to obey Him. This seems like circular reasoning, and it is, but to jump out of that cycle, we must define what being obedient to and loving God means. We do just that in this lesson.

The Foundational Truth

To love God means to be obedient to receive the Gospel and follow His commands.

Jesus gave His followers two commandments about love. The first and greatest commandment is to love God. If we love God, we trust Him and believe what He says. Therefore, to receive the Gospel and believe that Jesus is who He says He is and did what He says He did is for us to love Him. Additionally, to obey God when He tells us to do something is an act of love.

In this lesson, we see that, overwhelmingly, the New Testament Scriptures about obedience speak about obedience to two main things: obedience to the faith, which means to receive the Gospel by faith and remain in that faith, and obedience to God. There are some verses about obedience to authorities, parents, masters, and husbands, but most of the discussion in the New Testament about obedience concerns our submission to the Gospel of Grace and the commands of Jesus.

Obedience to the Faith

In the New Testament, we see a few different explanations of to whom or what we are to be obedient. The most common use of the word defined as *to obey* or *be obedient* refers to obeying the faith or the truth of the Gospel. It simply means **to believe**.

Read **1 John 3:23**. What are the two commandments John mentions in this verse?

Read **Romans 1:5**. What does Paul say we are to be obedient to in this verse?

Read **Romans 6:16-17**. Verse 16 says that before we are found in Christ, we were slaves of sin which leads to death. This refers to our spiritual and eternal death. The obedience Paul refers to here leads to righteousness. You received that because you obeyed from the heart what?

What doctrine must Paul have been talking about?

Read **Romans 16:17**. Those who were causing divisions and offenses were contrary to what?

Read **Romans 16:18**. Was Paul speaking about believers?   Yes   No

How do you know?

Read **Romans 16:19**. The Romans' obedience had become known to all. Taking into consideration the context of this verse, what do you think they were being obedient about?

Read **Romans 16:25-26**. What is Jesus able to establish you according to?

For obedience to what?

Read **Acts 6:7**. As the Word of God was spreading, there were many priests who became obedient to what?

Read **2 Corinthians 9:12-13**. Speaking about giving, Paul mentions that the saints glorified God for the Corinthians' obedience of their confession to what?

There are a couple scriptures that mention those who do not obey the Word or the Gospel.

Read **2 Thessalonians 1:1-10**. Who will Jesus take vengeance on according to verse 8?

Read **1 Peter 2:6-8**. Who are those who are disobedient?

Notice the contrast between those who believe and those who are disobedient. In English, *belief* and *disobedience* are not exactly opposites. We typically think that belief refers to how we think, and disobedience refers to what we do. In English, we might expect verse 7 to say *believe* and *don't believe* or *obedient* and *disobedient* to have consistent opposites. The issue with this verse is that the Greek word translated here as *disobedient* means both *unbelief* and *disobedience*. (As I mentioned in chapter one, *Jesus*.) For English readers, this translation is confusing, misleading, and legalistic. This anti-grace interpretation speaks of the need for better behavior instead of simple faith. If you read this passage with the word *unbelief* in place of *disobedient* it not only makes sense for the sentence but also for the context of the entire passage.

Reread **1 Peter 2:7** and use the words *don't believe* in place of *disobedient*.

We see, then, that we are to be obedient to the Gospel, faith, or to believe. When we put our faith in the grace and righteousness of Jesus for our own righteousness, we are obedient to the Gospel or the faith. Our salvation was Jesus' mission, and when we receive it by faith, that means we trust Him and love Him in return. Obeying God first means receiving the truth of the Gospel of Grace and continuing in that faith.

Read **Colossians 1:21-23**. What did Paul tell the Colossians to continue in?

And what should they not be moved away from?

Once we put our faith in the Gospel of Grace, what then? How should we view obedience between the time we profess Jesus and the end of our earthly lives? How do we *live* or *walk* in obedience to God? Let's find out.

Obedience to God

Being obedient to God is foundational in our walk with Him. There are different ways we can obey God, and I will categorize them for you into two types: direct commands from God and loving one another. In this lesson, we examine the first type, and we will address the second type in the next lesson.

Let's begin by looking at the often-referenced scripture about obedience. It is found in the Old Testament.

Read **1 Samuel 15:22**. Speaking to Saul, what did Samuel say was better than sacrifice?

Saul was getting ready to offer sacrifices to the LORD as an act of worship for his victory (*1 Samuel 15:15*) when Samuel confronted him. Samuel reminded Saul that he was given a direct command from the LORD God to "utterly destroy" the Amalekites and Saul disobeyed that command (*1 Samuel 15:18-19*). Then Samuel said what we read in verse 22 above about obedience versus sacrifice.

To love God is to obey Him. Saul lost his kingdom because of this disobedience.

It is concerning that this verse is often used out of context for believers today. People present it out of context to make a general statement about obedience. They don't clearly state that Saul's disobedience was in defiance of a direct command by the LORD and, therefore, his act of worship through sacrifice was pretentious.

This vague presentation of obedience draws people into shame about their own lives as they contemplate and worry about what they have done that God would declare as disobedient. They might think, *"Maybe I shouldn't go worship at church because I did some stuff that God probably thinks wasn't good enough. After all, God desires obedience, not sacrifice."*

I have mentioned this before; this vague message of obedience is a cloak for legalism.

Understanding the context of this passage is important. This passage should not be used to condemn people and guilt them into some form of ill-defined obedience. Rather, this passage teaches us that if you receive a direct command from God, you will obey that command if you love Him.

Another example of this idea, found in Acts chapter nine, concerns another man named Saul.

> Read *Acts 9:1-20*. Both Saul (also known as Paul) and Ananias heard a direct command from the Lord Jesus, and they obeyed His command. What were Jesus' commands to them, and how did they respond?

There are many more examples in the Word of God that show people being obedient to God's direct commands. These are great examples for us to see that when God calls us specifically to do, say, or go, we can trust that He has a plan, it's important, and He wants us to obey. You never know, like with Paul, God might have a global strategy in place that He is asking us to participate in!

When and if God commands us to do something, we will do it because we love Him. But how do we know what God commands us to do? Our examples were of people who heard directly from God or through one of His prophets. Audibly hearing from God can happen anytime, but it isn't the most common way God communicates with us, and hearing from a prophet of God is rare these days. The writer of Hebrews tells us that God now speaks to us by His Son (See **Hebrews 1:1-2**). The primary way we hear God is through His Word and through His Spirit.

God desires us to obey Him, but what does that obedience look like? Can we make a list of things we are to do? And is that list for everyone? Is your list the same as mine? As you pray and read the Bible, be sensitive to the Spirit's guidance. Jesus' commandments are to love, so everything we think God asks us to do must be loving. If it isn't loving, it can't be from God.

"Let all that you do be done with love."

1 Corinthians 16:14 NKJV

Why Does it Matter to You?

Why does it matter that you understand what it means to love God? How might that change your life and approach to your relationship with Him?

Why it Matters to Grace

The definition of loving God we learned in this lesson makes us part of the New Covenant. Your love for God manifests through your belief in God and His Gospel of Grace and your trust in Jesus for your righteousness. That act of faith is your first action of obedience to God. Furthermore, you will exhibit your love for God through doing what He asks of you, whether it is something specific, or simply loving others. God's grace means He loves you and welcomes you into His kingdom because of your faith, not because you successfully check off some godly to-dos. You enter His radical grace through your obedience to the Gospel.

Confirm the Brick

Are you ready to declare that loving God means that you are obedient to the faith for salvation and to specific things He asks of you? If yes, put your check mark next to the foundational truth below.

Yes, to love God means to be obedient to receive the Gospel and to His direct commands.

Love One Another
Brick 24

"But concerning brotherly love you have no need that I should write to you,
for you yourselves are taught by God to love one another."

1 Thessalonians 4:9

Jesus gave us two simple commands: love God and love one another. In the previous lesson, we discovered that to love God means to believe His Gospel and obey His direct commands. In this lesson, we examine Jesus' second command to love one another.

Though Jesus' commands are simple to say, they are not simple to do in our flesh. However, we are not of the flesh if we are in Christ; we are of the Spirit, and when the Spirit gets involved, love happens. We fulfill Jesus' first command to love God when we put our faith in Him and receive His gospel message. We fulfill His second command when we love others, and we do that because we love God.

Our new identity in Christ is the new man or woman He created us to be. Our new self has been released from striving to be obedient to a list of dos and don'ts and freed to simply love others. Loving others seems impossible sometimes, but when we approach love in our spirit and submit to God's Spirit, it isn't burdensome and is possible (*1 John 5:3*).

The Foundational Truth

We can fulfill Jesus' commandment to love one another through the power of His Spirit.

Jesus gave us the command to love others, including our enemies. Love of others seems impossible until you understand that God gave us the Spirit so we can achieve the impossible. The Word tells us that with God, all things are possible (*Mark 9:23*). Love for others is generated in our lives when we submit to the Spirit and fully embrace God's radical grace.

Many Bible teachers talk about loving others. Sadly, though, they leave this command hanging out there with no honest answer as to how we are supposed to accomplish this seemingly impossible command. Our dualism provides us with the answer. We cannot love others the way God wants us to if we walk in our flesh or view others in their flesh. We can only succeed in love if we allow our new spiritual nature to take control of our lives and submit to the Holy Spirit. He provides us with the fruit of love that we may offer to those around us. The Bible teaches us what love is and what love looks like when it is put into action.

Love Is

As we begin our study about loving one another, we will start with what the Word says about love. There is no possibility that we will ever be able to define love fully because it is multifaceted and divine.

Read *1 John 4:8*. He who does not love does not what?

It must be true, then, that He who knows God does what?

God is what?

Now you know why we can never truly define love. God is love, and we will never be able to wrap our minds around all that God is. However, we can begin to gain some understanding of love as we dig into the Word and see what love does when we put it into action.

Love Does

Jesus renewed our hearts and sent His Spirit to produce His fruit in us, then commanded us to love one another. He gave us the ability to love. God gave us the goods to love the way He always intended. He freed us from everything that held us back from loving one another, loving our neighbor, and even loving our enemy.

Love is both an emotion and an action. We can feel love for others like our spouses, children, grandchildren, and friends. When we love someone, our actions will align with that inner emotion of love. Love becomes action.

The Word tells us that if we are in Christ, we will love one another.

Read *John 13:35*. Speaking to His disciples, how did Jesus say people would know that they were His disciples?

Read *1 John 4:12*. If we love one another, we know what two things are true?

Read *Ephesians 5:1-2* As we walk in love, we are imitators of whom?

What does love in action look like? I cannot tell you what it will look like specifically, as the Spirit might lead you to love in a million different ways. But the Word does give us a picture of what love in action might look like. Let's see what love does and does not do.

Read *1 Corinthians 13:4-8*. This passage explains sixteen things that love does and some things love does not do. List them here.

This list is not meant to condemn you when you read it. This list is a mirror for you to see if you are aligned with the heart of God and walking in love or your flesh. Love is the measure by which we know we are walking in the Spirit.

Let's look at some other verses to see what love looks like.

Read *1 Peter 1:22*. How does this verse describe the way we love one another?

Read *Ephesians 4:1-2*. How do we love others?

Read *1 Peter 3:8-9*. What does love look like in this passage?

Read *1 Peter 4:8*. What kind of love are we to have?

These verses give us a snapshot of what love can look like. Many of us have no problem putting love into action when we have an emotional attachment to someone, but what about those hard-to-love people, the people we don't really know, those who have hurt us, or whom we call our enemies?

Let's see what Jesus said.

Read *Matthew 5:44*. Love whom?

Bless whom?

Do good to whom?

Pray for whom?

By the grace of God and the power of His Spirit, we can love, bless, do good, and pray for anyone, no matter who they are to us. When we look at people with our spiritual eyes closed, we see their failures, flaws, and flesh. We emphasize their wrongdoings without seeing them as a creation of God who suffers and struggles just like we do. There is a fascinating verse I'd like you to look at next.

Read *2 Corinthians 5:16*. Paul explained that we now regard, or view no one according to what?

It is difficult to love others when we view them according to their flesh. However, when we see them as spiritual beings with souls who need saving or are overwhelmed by their sinful flesh, we can foster compassion for them.

Loving them means admitting they have value to God, recognizing their value leads to compassion, and compassion can lead to forgiveness if you seek it.

Yes, I did mean to put it in that order. You might think forgiveness should come before love and compassion, but I submit that you must understand someone's value to God and love them as God's creation before you can truly forgive them. Forgiveness is born of love.

Jesus told us that we can love anyone and everyone. He commanded us to love. We will love others in various ways every day. Love can be revealed during an argument, as you serve your community or family, when talking to a stranger, or while wiping someone's tears away. To love others, you must reach into the Spirit's well of fruit and see the world through the spiritual eyes and heart that Jesus has given you. To love is to walk according to the Spirit and in His radical grace.

Finally, read *1 Corinthians 16:14*. Do everything with what?

Why Does it Matter?

Why is it important that you know that to obey Jesus means to love one another? Does this definition change your view of the word *disobedience* according to the Gospel? How does loving others speak to your appreciation for God's radical grace?

Why it Matters to Grace

Knowing that Jesus' command was to love others shows us that God is all about love. God's character is love, and His desire for us is to love. Once we realize that He is all about love, we can see that radical grace is true and real, and we can both receive it for ourselves and offer it to others. Love is God's motivation for His grace, and we can love others by His grace. Love and grace are two peas from the same pod.

Confirm the Brick

Do you agree that you are now capable of loving others, including your enemies, through the power of the Holy Spirit? If you believe this is true, place a check by the statement below.

Yes, I can fulfill Jesus' command to love others through the grace and power of His Spirit.

Build the Foundation of Radical Grace

It is time to cement these *Love* bricks into your foundation of radical grace. Loving others is a work of your spiritual nature as you walk in your new and true identity in Christ. Love produces life, reconciliation, relationship, forgiveness, peace, and joy. God's gift of grace gave you the power and opportunity to love those who cross your path. Place these *Love* bricks as capstones on your foundation of radical grace.

Bricks 22, 23, and 24: *Love*

The facts:

Jesus' new commandments are to love God and to love one another.

To love God means to be obedient to receive the Gospel and to be obedient to His commands.

We can fulfill Jesus' commandment to love one another through the grace and power of His Spirit.

Remember, once in place, the bricks are unshakable.

Live Free and Unashamed

Your new life in Jesus allows you the freedom to release the condemnation of not measuring up. You are free to love God and serve Him in the ways He inspires you.

There are a couple ways you can apply this lesson to your everyday life. First, I encourage you to notice all the seemingly insignificant ways and times you love someone. Do this for a few days. You will notice that you probably live out God's commands more than you thought. And second, notice the times when you are not loving. In those moments, remember that you can flick on your Light switch and walk in your spirit instead of your flesh. Sometimes, that is a challenging request, but the Spirit is with you to help.

The whole point of understanding Jesus' commandments for the New Covenant is for you to walk in His grace and be obedient to Him in that grace. Therefore, allow yourself to fail without condemnation, to get back up and keep walking, and to let the love of God, which He poured into your heart, pour over the people around you as you impart His radical grace to them.

Part 2

Unshakable Foundation

"Whoever comes to Me, and hears My sayings and does them, I will show you whom he is like: He is like a man building a house, who dug deep and laid the foundation on the rock. And when the flood arose, the stream beat vehemently against that house, and could not shake it, for it was founded on the rock."

Luke 6:47-48

Chapter 9

Freedom

"Therefore if the Son makes you free, you shall be free indeed."

John 8:36

You have carefully examined all the bricks that make up the foundation of radical grace. You have built a strong foundation that gives you a sure footing for your walk in Jesus and bolsters your faith and relationship with Him. As much as you feel accomplished in all you have learned, you might have a few more questions. That's okay. Most people do. For example, you might have some of the following questions.

"Yeah, but what about sin? Does grace mean that it's okay to keep on sinning?"
"Yeah, but saying we are free in Jesus can't mean we can just do whatever we want?"
"Yeah, but doesn't radical grace mean you believe in cheap grace?"

My husband, Phillip, and I receive a lot of *"yeah, buts"* when we talk about grace with people. What does freedom in the grace of Jesus mean, exactly? How can we reconcile the above questions while maintaining the integrity and purity of our stance on God's radical grace?

In this chapter, we dig into our freedom in Jesus. I will address the above questions and provide solid, clear answers so you can send those *yeah buts* packing once and for all. The main difficulty in receiving this lesson is that we all come to this topic with years of confusing and false baggage. Set that baggage aside for this discussion and allow yourself to consider that grace means that you are 100% free in Christ. Grace is not only for your eternal salvation but for every moment you remain here on earth and it frees you from making your sin the emphasis of your faith in Jesus. Our goal is to explore our freedom of choice, the cost and value of our freedom, and the freedom to walk according to the Spirit, in love.

Read chapters 17-18 of *Radical Grace* if you are reading along with this study.

Freedom to Choose

"All things are lawful for me, but all things are not helpful. All things are lawful for me, but I will not be brought under the power of any."

1 Corinthians 6:11

God's grace means we are genuinely free. In this study, we have already laid the foundation that Jesus has freed us from striving to fulfill the Old Covenant Law. However, our freedom reaches beyond not having to satisfy the Law. Our freedom reaches into living with the freedom to walk in our flesh, a.k.a. unrighteousness, or walk in the Spirit, a.k.a. righteousness. God had to give us that choice for grace to be grace.

The concept of grace and how far we can take it has been debated, discussed, and deliberated since the time of Christ. How can one reconcile grace with sin? Some say that taking grace all the way means you are saying it is okay to keep sinning. This thinking is a misunderstanding of freedom in God's grace. Receiving radical grace shouldn't ever diminish the cost and consequences of sin. While the Bible teaches that sin is terrible, it also teaches that grace is 100% grace, which covers all our sins or it isn't grace at all. How do we reconcile these two?

God's grace is radical, offering us complete freedom. This freedom allows us to sin without losing our salvation, but it's crucial to understand that this doesn't make sin okay. Sin remains sin. If grace doesn't allow for the freedom to choose between righteous and unrighteous behavior, it ceases to be grace.

Let's dive into these questions by logically examining the facts.

Free Choice

God wants you to choose Him because He loves you.

Read *1 John 4:19*. Restate this verse in your own words.

I believe He didn't create us to love Him with built-in love like a robot because He wants us to choose Him of our own free will. That's the beauty of a relationship. We choose our people, and they choose us. That choice makes it precious. God loved us first, and then He died for us. He provided every reason for us not to reject Him and His love but to choose Him and to love Him back.

Read **Acts 13:44-46**. Like the Jews in this passage, you have a choice to accept or reject Jesus.

Our choice is one of the most precious gifts God has given us. It holds the power to make love special. Our freedom to choose God or not to choose God was the risk He was willing to take to foster an authentic relationship with us. He wants us to choose Him, but to make the choice valid, He had to give us the freedom not to choose Him.

Recall that in Christ, we still drag around our old fleshly sinful nature, but we gain a newly remodeled spiritual and righteous part as well. That part is our new identity, our authentic selves. My friends, you must understand that who you are in Christ is that new you. Jesus separated you from your old flesh; it died with Jesus on the cross, and you no longer need to identify as that sinful person.

> Read **Galatians 5:25**. This statement implies that we have a choice. What are the two different possible choices?

When we choose to walk in our flesh, we, our new spiritual and eternal self, submit our physical temporal bodies to our old sinful fleshly self. But since we live in the Spirit, we can instead choose to walk in Him. Sin tempts our old flesh, and we sometimes submit to that temptation, which can have harmful consequences for us and those around us. However, when we choose to ignore that old self and walk in the Spirit, we submit our bodies and minds to righteous works, which will produce good consequences.

We don't choose to walk in either one continuously; we walk in our flesh and the spirit off and on. Even so, whether we walk in the spirit or the flesh, our new nature is always righteous because Jesus made it so. While we might fluctuate from flesh to spirit, our righteousness never wavers. Our new identity doesn't change or lose any righteousness. Additionally, everything we do is holy when we walk in that new spirit. Those holy works can't be tarnished or diminished by our carnal self or fleshly works.

Free to Sin

Have you heard questions like the following?

"Yeah, but what about sin?"

"Does God's grace mean that people can just keep on sinning?"

These are the questions that push the limits and help us see that God's grace is truly radical.

The key to answering these questions is *righteousness*.

Remember, your behavior doesn't determine your righteousness and holiness; they are obtained by Jesus giving them to you. They don't ebb and flow. They don't grow or diminish. They don't appear then disappear, strengthen then weaken, or exist then vanish. Once you are made holy and righteous, and as you continue in faith that you are, they will never waver, get better, get worse, or disappear based on your behavior.

If these things are true, then the answer to the question about sin is:

Yes, if you sin as a follower of Jesus, you will still be loved by God, not lose your salvation, and still be righteous and holy.

This radical truth is what defines God's grace.

Let's be honest, we *do* still sin. The key is understanding that God doesn't impute our sin, He doesn't put it on our account, if we are in Christ. Paul addressed the very question we are exploring.

Read **Galatians 2:15-21**. This section of Galatians is powerful.

Paul is saying that sin is defined by transgression, or breaking God's Law.

Read **Romans 4:15**. Where there is no law, there is no what?

Paul is telling us that sin isn't accounted for if there is no law. Remember, Jesus fulfilled the Law and ended the requirement to fulfill it for those who are in Him.

Therefore, if we restore or re-establish the Law by placing ourselves back into submission to it in an attempt to stop sinning, we are denying who Jesus is and what He did for us. If we do this, we declare that our righteousness depends not on Jesus but on our behavioral obedience, which is useless because we can never achieve the perfect righteousness that God requires. Since the Scripture tells us that the Law cannot bring righteousness (**Romans 3:20**), submitting to it makes Jesus' death and resurrection meaningless.

The truth is our righteousness **depends only** on Jesus and the grace of God. We are no longer under the Law but under grace, which we mustn't set aside. Thus, if we sin while in Christ, our righteousness is not affected because it comes from Jesus, not from our obeying any rules or laws.

If I say we cannot lose our salvation or righteousness if we sin, does that mean I am saying that sin is *"okay"*? No. That is not what I am saying at all. Hang in there, as I will explain this further in the next lesson.

Before we move on, recall what John said about sin.

Read ***1 John 5:16-17***. What are the two types of sin John mentioned here?

What is the only sin that can lead to death?

If we sin by not believing in the grace of Jesus, the consequence is eternal death. However, if we sin in anything else, that sin does not lead to eternal death because our righteousness does not depend on our actions; it comes from Jesus.

Read ***1 John 2:1***. Who is our Advocate?

God allowed us to make choices to have an authentic relationship with Him. He was willing to take the risk of us abusing that freedom so that we could freely choose Him. Love is worth the risk.

Why Does it Matter to You?

Why does it matter that you are given free choice by God? How does your freedom of choice personally affect your life and relationship with Jesus?

Why it Matters to Grace

Our choice to receive His Son or to reject Him reveals the magnificence and glory of God's grace. His grace allows us to receive Him without forcing us into a relationship we do not want. He loves us and desires us to choose Him, but to have that happen, He had to allow the option of denial. Jesus risked all to gain those who would come through His radical grace.

The Cost vs. the Value of Grace

"For you were bought at a price; therefore glorify God in your body and in your spirit, which are God's."

1 Corinthians 6:20

In the last lesson, we concluded that, as followers of Jesus, we **can** sin and not lose our salvation or our standing with God. Our salvation isn't based on us not sinning, so it cannot be lost if we sin. We **can** go on sinning and still be righteous and saved, but **should** we? Because of this freedom, can we say sin is *"okay"*?

Is Sin Okay?

Define *"Okay"*

I would ask the following questions to people who want to say that sin is *"okay"* because of grace.

"Okay, in what way?"
"Okay for you because God won't punish you?"
"Okay, for the people you hurt by your sin?"
"Okay for God because He doesn't care about you or the people you hurt?"
"What do you want to justify?"

Yes, as a true believer in Jesus, your sin won't send you to Hell, but sin will never be *"okay."* Sin is what drove Jesus to suffer a terrible beating and to die on the cross. Sin carries consequences for you and those around you. So yes, if you are a believer in Jesus, God won't condemn you to Hell for cussing out the store clerk, lusting after your secretary, or lying to your mom about where you are going. Still, I think it breaks God's heart when we don't consider how our sin damages relationships, hurts others, and causes devastating consequences in our own and others' lives.

Though God doesn't condemn us for our sins, that doesn't mean that the consequences aren't real and that our sins don't affect us and others. That is why Peter and Paul told us not to use our freedom to excuse sin.

154

Read *1 Peter 2:15-16*. Speaking of our liberty, or freedom, what does Peter exhort us not to do?

Read *Galatians 5:13*. Paul speaks about our liberty in a similar way. What does he say about it?

Read *1 Corinthians 6:12*. All things are what? Not all things are what?

If Peter and Paul encouraged us not to use our freedom for our flesh, they believed we had a choice. However, they also understood the consequences of using our freedom for selfish gain and urged us to consider not doing so. Paul declared that he would not be brought under the power of anything. His example can inspire us.

Paul's further explanation clarifies that his words are not meant to encourage sin but to highlight God's grace and focus on our new life in Jesus. Let's examine a passage that explains this concept.

Read *Romans 6:1-2*. Paul told us no; we shouldn't continue in sin. Look at his reasoning.

We died to what?

How will we what?

Read *Romans 6:3-4*. We were baptized into his what?

We should walk in what?

Read *Romans 6:5*. We carry the likeness of Christ in what two ways?

Read *Romans 6:6-11*. Briefly summarize this passage.

We have covered this topic before, but I would like you to think about it in the context of sin. This passage tells us that Jesus separated our old man or woman, the perpetrator of sin, from our new spiritual nature.

Read ***Romans 6:12***. We don't have to obey what?

Read ***Romans 6:13***. What choice do we have?

Read ***Romans 6:14***. Why doesn't sin have dominion over us?

Therefore, the question isn't what we do about sin but what we do now with our new life in Christ. Radical grace means we may turn our attention away from our old selves because that old person has lost control and move forward with our hearts and minds on what we can now do in the spirit with help from the Holy Spirit. That is the freedom that God's grace has given us.

The point is, when we walk in our flesh, our new nature's righteousness and holiness don't change, and sin can't affect or diminish who we are in Christ. But in our flesh, sin can cause all sorts of harmful consequences. God desires for us to have a more peaceful and loving life. Sin doesn't allow that.

We see then why Peter and Paul mention that, while we are free, we shouldn't decide to use our freedom to keep sinning. It is a matter of the heart. This relationship between sin and grace means that life is messy; we will sin, and we will do great and loving things, but either way, God still loves us.

Because sin is paid for through God's grace, that doesn't make it *"okay."* Sin is still sin.

Sin is, at best, a dissipation of our time and effort, and at worst, damaging and destructive.

Grace is not an excuse to get away with stuff. But at the same time, we are His even though we have our sinful flesh hanging around. Grace says Jesus loves us that much. He died and rose again so that we could grab hold of His radical grace one hundred percent and live in the liberty that Peter and Paul talk about.

Your relationship with God is personal. If you are His, you have the Spirit living in you. Allow the Spirit to speak to your heart about this matter and let Him lead. Remember, when you are walking in the Spirit, you can't fulfill your flesh. It is time the church stops emphasizing our old fleshly self of sin and turns her attention toward the new life in Jesus that He so graciously provides for us.

I would like to mention something very important before we go on. Grace is not a cloak to cover up or excuse abuse. If you are in a situation where you are being told to stay with someone who is abusing you, and that you should have grace with them or you are not a good Christian, get to a safe place, and don't let anyone tell you it is ungodly to escape abuse. Get to safety, then you can talk to God about how to deal with your abuser in a godly way.

Devaluing the Gift

An incorrect understanding of how grace and sin relate causes some strange doctrines. I have heard people say that if you fully receive God's grace and don't sacrifice and work hard on your sin, then you are taking grace for granted and that you think grace is cheap.

Taking Grace for Granted

To people who say believers in radical grace are taking it for granted, I say, *"Yep, I am. God freely **granted** me His grace and asked me to **take** it."*

If we don't fully receive it as **free**, then we might believe that we can do something to deserve it. But as we've learned, no one will ever deserve God's grace, no matter what they do. We need to let ourselves receive it without needing to earn it. Instead of finding reasons to feel guilty, listen to grace when it says, *"I love you."* God's grace is unconditional, it's not something we can earn. Jesus grants it, and we take it. Period.

Additionally, for those who refuse God's grace simply because some people use it as an excuse to sin, I would use an old idiom, *"Don't throw the baby out with the bath water."* You don't know whether people are saved or not. Only God knows that. Don't miss out on the overwhelming blessing of living in God's grace because of what you see others doing. Let God deal with them while you grab hold of His grace and enjoy the blessings it brings.

Grace Isn't Cheap

Grace isn't cheap. The word cheap implies it costs something; not much, but something. It did cost Jesus everything, but us? Nope. It doesn't cost us anything. It isn't cheap, it's FREE. Grace is both totally free and extremely costly, but its cost to us doesn't imply its value. Grace is infinitely valuable, a priceless gift that shows how much we are cherished and loved by God.

The only way to cheapen or devalue the gift of grace is not to receive it. For example, let's say you worked hard to save enough money to buy a car for your child. After giving it to them, they never drove it or acknowledged the gift. The reason they parked the car doesn't matter. It doesn't matter if they feel unworthy or can't believe you offered them a gift without any strings attached. The point is that, for some reason, they didn't use the gift given to them.

First, your child not using the car doesn't inherently devalue the gift. Second, wouldn't you feel as if *they* didn't value the car? Or that they have cheapened it in their minds? Third, how would you feel? God's priceless gift of grace, though it cost Him everything, was free to us. Its inherent value is never lost, but we can diminish its value in our lives if we don't fully receive it and use it.

When Jesus gave us the gift of the Gospel and bestowed His grace upon us, He knew we would still sin. He knew about our sinful nature, yet He still died for us. He knew we might choose to do unrighteous things, but He still chose to make us righteous so we could be with Him. He still chose to offer His incredible gift of grace to us without any expectations or requirements of us. That isn't cheap grace; that is radical grace, a profound and transformative grace that inspires us to live a life of freedom and joy that reflects its value.

Grace Cost Jesus Everything

What is the value of grace? I'd say it is infinitely valuable. It is impossible to put a value on God's grace. It cost God everything to give us His grace.

Read *John 15:13*. What did Jesus do for His friends?

Read *Matthew 27:50*. What does this verse describe?

Read *1 Corinthians 6:20*. What price did Jesus pay to purchase you?

Jesus paid the price of His life to purchase all of humanity. How valuable is His life? I don't believe we can even answer that question.

Grace, the ultimate gift, is truly free. It cannot be earned through our works, nor can it be deserved. This grace, given to us without condition, blesses us with the freedom to choose to walk in our new natures, to walk in love, and to walk hand-in-hand with Jesus, whose love reveals the immeasurable value He places on us.

Why Does it Matter to You?

Why must you understand that though Jesus paid a great price to offer His grace, you do not need to pay anything? Fully receiving God's grace doesn't mean you are diminishing the impact of sin or the value of grace. Does this fact change your view of radical grace?

Why it Matters to Grace

Jesus knows we still have sinful flesh that will fail sometimes, and that sin is destructive and harmful, yet He died to separate us from the power of sin. He gave us what we need to set our feet toward walking in love and living by the Spirit. Jesus paid the costly price to bring us into His family and gave us the freedom to choose to walk in His love instead of our sinful nature. What Jesus has done defines grace. His free but valuable gift of grace can only be devalued by our not fully receiving it and not confidently walking in it. That is radical grace.

Free Like the Wind

"The wind blows where it wishes, and you hear the sound of it, but cannot tell where it comes from and where it goes. So is everyone who is born of the Spirit."

John 3:8

In the last lesson, we learned that sin is not *"okay,"* but how do we know what to do if we don't have a list of dos and don'ts to follow? We trust the Spirit. Our new life in Christ means we can live by the Spirit and make love the basis of everything we do. Each situation we face becomes an opportunity to do the loving thing. Every situation in our lives won't have a *do this* or *don't do that* note attached, but with the guidance of the Spirit, we can choose love, and that will never be the wrong answer.

Spiritual Choices

Though we don't get a list of dos and don'ts, we can make good, godly, and spiritual choices by considering how our actions affect others. Rather than deciding what is and is not sin, we can make love the goal and let the Spirit show us how to accomplish it.

I'm pretty sure most people who claim to be followers of Jesus aren't going around killing people, stealing from others, or worshipping a false god. Those types of sin we find easy to define as *"not okay."* But what about something less egregious? For example, is it okay to eat cake? Let's look at some possible scenarios for eating cake and see if we can define it as *"okay"* or *"not okay."*

For these examples, I am given the law: **You may have only one slice of cake**.

160

How much cake? One slice. I hadn't eaten for days because I was trapped inside my basement and no one found me until they came over to celebrate my birthday with me, cake in hand. Is it okay that I ate it?

How much cake? Once slice. Mom made it to celebrate my dad's birthday tomorrow. It just looked good, and I wanted it. Is it okay that I ate it?

How much cake? One slice. My daughter is a baker and wanted me to try her new cake recipe. I wanted to encourage her, so I tasted it. Is it okay that I ate it? It was delicious, by the way.

How much cake? One slice. It was the last slice of cake from my sister's wedding cake that she and her husband had saved from their wedding two years ago. He passed away last year, and she was going to eat it to celebrate their love, as a memorial to him, but I ate it anyway. Is it okay that I ate it?

How much cake? One slice. It's my birthday, I haven't had cake since my last birthday, and I enjoyed every bite as I celebrated with my family. Is it okay that I ate it?

How much cake? One slice. Tomorrow is my birthday, and I haven't had cake since my last birthday. My sister made it as a surprise for me and couldn't wait to see my reaction to seeing it. I am supposed to enjoy it tomorrow as I celebrate with my family, but I didn't want to wait, so I snuck into the refrigerator and cut out a piece. Is it okay that I ate it? She did a great job, by the way.

I admit these examples vary in degrees of stupidity, but you get the point.

Yes, I technically obeyed the law and ate only one slice, but the consequences of my actions in some of these scenarios may be hurtful to others. The cake-eating dilemma is not as simple as it seems.

We can see that the answer to the question, *"Is it okay to eat cake?"* varies depending on many factors: the circumstances, others whom it will affect if I do, how much I eat, who owns the cake, and even the timing of eating it. No one could write a law that would address every scenario and circumstance in life. The answers to some questions aren't always black and white, so having a set list of dos and don'ts doesn't work. Life is messy. This truth is why we need the Holy Spirit.

Here are some scripture verses that give us some idea of when something is sinful.

Re-read *1 John 5:17*. All what is sin?

Read *Romans 14:23*. Whatever is not from what is sin?

Jesus sent the Holy Spirit to come live in us so He could help us discern the difference.

Read *John 3:8*. What does this verse say about those who are born of the Spirit?

What does that mean?

If we are born of the Spirit, He helps us discern right from wrong or righteousness and unrighteousness. There is freedom in not having everything written down on paper about whether you can do something or not, because each moment of every day is unique for every child of God. This freedom is a powerful gift, but it also comes with the hope that we will make choices that align with God's love.

The beauty of our faith lies in the fact that Jesus' grace is radical enough to handle both our righteousness and our unrighteousness. If we love God, though, we will seek to cause no harm. Sure, we will mess that up sometimes, but we will keep leaning toward love. If our obedience to God is to love Him and love others, then love is always the measure by which we know something won't cause harm. It isn't loving to cuss out the store clerk, lust after your secretary, or lie to your mom about where you are going. Like I said before, we won't be condemned to Hell for doing so, but if we love God, we will care about whether we hurt others.

Free to Care

Love means we care about the consequences of our actions not because we might suffer or get caught, but because we care about how our actions affect other people. We still slip up sometimes, but as a transformed, Spirit-filled, God-loving, Jesus-believing, righteous new creation, somewhere deep down in our innermost being, we care about others. Caring about what we do is not about whether we sin or not, and is not a salvation issue, but it is about living in the new life that Jesus has given us and allowing His Spirit to lead us in loving others.

I will conclude this part of the discussion with the following verses.

Read *John 8:47*. Those who are of God hear what?

Read *John 13:35*. How will all know that one is a disciple of Jesus?

Read *1 John 3:10*. How can one tell the children of God from the children of the devil?

Read *1 John 3:14*. One who doesn't love his or her brother abides in what?

Read *1 John 3:17*. What example is given that shows someone who doesn't have the love of God in them?

Read *1 John 4:12-16*. God's love abides in us who do what?

Read *1 John 4:20-21*. If one loves God, they will love whom?

Once you are transformed and made new in your spirit, that doesn't mean you will never sin again in the flesh. If you think you won't, you will be gravely ashamed and disappointed in yourself. Wallowing in shame and self-hatred is not freedom. Those whom Christ sets free are free indeed (*John 8:36* NKJV). When you fail, flip that Light switch back on and try again. Radical grace says you can lay that shame and condemnation down and start fresh the very next second.

Read *1 Corinthians 15:34*. What are we to awake to?

What does Paul mean by this verse?

While grace pays for our sins and makes us righteous, it doesn't rid us of our ability to choose sin because we still have our flesh hanging around. Meanwhile, sin is still sin; it's not okay. At the same time, Jesus has forgiven all our past, present, and future sins. Additionally, God said to love one another. These statements are all accurate simultaneously, and their diverse truths are why we need the Spirit to guide us in righteousness and God's radical grace.

Why Does it Matter to You?

Why is it essential that you recognize that as a child of God you are free to let the Spirit guide you in every situation? Does that extent of freedom make you uneasy? Why or why not?

Why it Matters to Grace

God gave us the freedom and ability to choose Him or not, to choose to sin or not, and to choose love or not. Just think about how God must feel when we choose Him and choose to love others! God took the risk to give us freedom in the Spirit. He knew some of us would not choose to walk in love, but He gave us that choice anyway for the good of those who would choose it and what that would do for the world. That is what grace is all about. His grace is that radical.

Chapter 10

Gospel of Radical Grace

"And you, who were alienated and enemies in your mind by wicked works, yet now he has reconciled in the body of His flesh through death, to present you holy, and blameless, and above reproach in His sight – if indeed you continue in the faith, grounded and steadfast, and are not moved away from the hope of the gospel which you heard, which was preached to every creature under heaven, of which I, Paul, became a minister."

Colossians 1:21-23

In chapters 1-8, you studied the overwhelming evidence of God's grace. In this study, you weeded out some false doctrines and brought to light some of the poignant aspects of the true Gospel of Grace often lost in modern Christian teachings. It is time to put everything you have learned together in an organized fashion that describes the Radical Grace version of the Gospel.

Read chapters 19-21 of *Radical Grace* if you are reading along with this study.

The Gospel of Radical Grace

The Gospel of Radical Grace is a more complete picture of what Jesus has done for us than most versions I have seen. Any gospel message should be based on all the bricks covered in this study.

You can put your full faith and trust in this radical grace version of the Gospel.

The Romans Road of Radical Grace

As a review of what we have learned, we will look at the verses from the book of Romans that contain the good news of Jesus. I have included supporting verses for your further study. Also note the **bricks** that are relevant for each of the elements of the Gospel.

Brick: *Righteousness*

Because of Adam's sin, all of humanity is born into that sin and, therefore, born unrighteous. God's standard requires righteousness to inherit eternity.

Read **Romans 3:23**. All have what?

Read **Romans 3:9**. Who are under sin?

Read **Galatians 3:22**. Who has been confined under sin?

Brick: *Righteousness*

Because of sin, all of humanity is condemned and facing both physical and spiritual death.

Read **Romans 6:23**. What is the cost of sin?

Read **Matthew 25:41** and **46**. What is the consequence for the unrighteous?

Read **Romans 5:12**. What came through sin?

Bricks: *Jesus, Promise,* and *Righteousness*

God promised to send a Savior to pay the penalty for our sin, endure God's wrath for us, and then impute His righteousness to those who would believe in Him. That Savior is Jesus.

Read **Romans 5:8**. What did Christ do for us, even though He knew we are sinners?

Read **John 15:13**. Jesus did what for His friends?

Read **Romans 4:25**. Why was Jesus delivered up?

Bricks: **Jesus, Promise, Righteousness, Old Covenant,** and **New Covenant**

Jesus came to fulfill God's promise to send a Savior, to pay the penalty for our unrighteousness, to fulfill the Old Covenant, and initiate the New Covenant which is a covenant of faith and grace.

Read **Romans 10:9**. What must we do to be saved?

Read **Matthew 10:32**. If we confess Jesus before men, what will He do?

Read **Romans 10:13**. If we call on the name of the Lord, what will happen?

Bricks: **Jesus, Promise, Righteousness, Old Covenant,** and **New Covenant**

Once we realize we are unrighteous, we believe in and call on Jesus to receive His righteousness for salvation through His New Covenant.

Read **Romans 10:10**. What two things do we receive if we believe and confess the Lord Jesus?

Read **Romans 4:5**. To we who believe on Jesus, our faith is accounted for what?

Read **1 Thessalonians 5:9**. What do we obtain through our Lord Jesus Christ?

Bricks: **Jesus, Promise, Righteousness, Old Covenant, New Covenant, New You,** and **Spirit**

As a participant in the New Covenant through being born again, we receive the very righteousness of Jesus and Jesus sends us the Spirit as a guarantee of that salvation.

Read ***Romans 10:4***. What is Christ to the Law?

Read ***Philippians 3:8-9***. Our righteousness is from God by what?

Read ***Galatians 2:16***. By the works of the Law no flesh will be what?

Bricks: ***Jesus, Promise, Righteousness, Old Covenant, New Covenant, New You,*** and ***Spirit***

Jesus fulfilled the Old Covenant so that we who put our faith in His righteousness for our own may be born again and receive His righteousness through that faith. As New Covenant believers, our new spiritual nature is made righteous, and that new man or woman is not in bondage to sin and will not experience death. We have the Holy Spirit to help us walk in righteousness.

Read ***Romans 6:14***. Because we are under grace and not the Law, sin doesn't have what over us?

Read ***Romans 6:11***. We can take it into account that we are dead to what and we are alive to what?

Read ***Romans 6:6***. We are no longer slaves of what?

Bricks: ***Jesus, Promise, Righteousness, Old Covenant, New Covenant, New You,*** and ***Spirit***

As New Covenant believers who have been sanctified and justified by the Spirit through faith in Jesus, we are under grace, not the Law. The Law gave life to sin, but Jesus fulfilled the Law, nailed it to the cross, and the power of sin was crucified with it. By the power of the Spirit living in us, our new spiritual nature is no longer a slave to sin. We may put off that old nature and put on the new one. When we walk according to the Spirit, we can't be walking according to our flesh.

Read ***Romans 13:14***. Put on Jesus and make no provision for what?

Read *Ephesians 4:20-24*. In Christ we can put off what and put on what?

Read *Galatians 5:16*. When we walk in the Spirit, we won't fulfill the lusts of what?

Bricks: *Jesus, Promise, Righteousness, Old Covenant, New Covenant, New You, Spirit,* and *Love*

Now that we have been born anew and have the Spirit living in us, we have the choice to put on our new man or woman and walk in the Spirit. When we walk in the Spirit and walk in love, our flesh is not in control, nor can it be. We may enjoy the blessing of our new life in Christ.

Read *Romans 7:6*. We now serve in the newness of what?

Read *2 Corinthians 3:6*. The letter (Law) does what, but the Spirit does what?

Read *Romans 8:11*. What will the Spirit give life to?

Bricks: *Jesus, Promise, Righteousness, Old Covenant, New Covenant, New You, Spirit,* and *Love*

As followers of Jesus and members of the New Covenant with all its blessings, we have been given a new life in the Spirit. We no longer must strive to fulfill the old Law; we are free to walk in love and obey Jesus' new commands to love God and love one another.

Read *Romans 13:10*. What is the fulfillment of the Law?

Read *John 13:34*. What is the new commandment?

Read *Colossians 3:14*. Above all, put on what?

Bricks: *Jesus, Promise, Righteousness, Old Covenant, New Covenant, New You, Spirit,* and *Love*

Our new life is defined by our new nature, and we are in fellowship with the Spirit. He leads us in this new life Jesus has given us.

Read **Romans 8:4**. The law is fulfilled in those who walk according to what?

Read **Galatians 5:25**. If we live in the Spirit, let us also what?

Read **Romans 8:14**. Who are the sons (and daughters) of God?

Bricks: ***Jesus, Promise, Righteousness, Old Covenant, New Covenant, New You, Spirit,*** and ***Love***

When we choose to walk in our new nature and walk in love, according to the Spirit, we cannot break any laws. We have the choice to walk in our flesh or in our spirit. There is no law against love.

Read **Romans 8:5**. What do those who live according to the flesh set their minds on? And those who live according to the Spirit?

Read **Romans 8:6**. To be carnally minded is what? And to be spiritually minded is what two things?

Read **Colossians 3:1-2**. Set our minds on what?

Read **Philippians 4:8** which is another great verse for this concept.

The Gospel of Radical Grace differs in a few ways from the typical presentation of the Gospel. The radical grace version includes the following facts and scriptures that are not typically included in other Romans Road Gospels:

We are made righteous. Romans 10:10

We are no longer under the Law. Romans 10:4

Sin doesn't enslave us anymore. Romans 6:14

We may choose to walk in our spirit instead of walking in our flesh. Romans 13:14, Romans 7:6, Romans 8:5

Love is the fulfillment of the new commandments we are given by Jesus. Romans 13:10, Romans 8:4

How do you think these scriptures change the message of the Gospel that you have heard in the past?

Do you think these scriptures present a departure from a focus on your sin to a focus on your new life in Christ? If so, in what way?

The Bootstrap Gospel

When our kid hits a home run, our team wins the Super Bowl, or we get to enjoy our favorite band live in concert, we are on our feet, our arms are in the air, and a smile is on our faces. We are excited. We would do the same if we found out we won $200,000,000 in the lottery. Why aren't we just as excited about God's grace?

Most people don't present the Gospel as an exciting win, a joyous thing, or valuable beyond our imagination. We get inundated with a dreary gospel message oozing with shame, condemnation, and pressure to perform. I call this gospel the Bootstrap Gospel, or B.S. Gospel for short. I call it this because of the common phrase, *"Pull yourself up by your bootstraps,"* which encourages people to pull themselves out of a difficult situation by mustering up some guts and grit and not relying on anyone else. This B.S. Gospel is so prevalent that I must bring it up in this chapter so you can stay clear of this teaching.

In many conversations with various people, I have noticed that when they speak about their faith or relationship with Jesus, they say things like the following:

"Yeah, Jesus died for my sins, but I have made some terrible choices in my past and have hurt people."

"I'm a Christian; I know Jesus died for my sins, but I can't seem to do the right stuff and live like a real Christian."

"I believe in Jesus; He died for my sins, and I am going to heaven."

Do you see anything missing from these people's description of the Gospel? Their understanding of the Gospel puts Jesus on the cross and buries Him in the tomb, but it doesn't mention His resurrection, their baptism of the Spirit, or their new life, not to mention hope, peace, joy, freedom, or any excitement at all.

I believe that is because the gospel we often hear emphasizes our sin and our work to correct it, devalues or excludes the Spirit's ministry in our lives, and neglects the beauty of our newly made spirit.

Because the B.S. Gospel centers on working to become more Christlike through works of the flesh, it is legalistic, which means it isn't a gospel of grace. The teachers of this message place burdensome rules and regulations on their listeners in the name of obedience. These rules don't produce righteous living; they create shame, guilt, and depression. This type of doctrine is a Jesus plus gospel, which is no gospel at all. This principle of working on your righteousness places your focus on your sin all the time, which puts you back in the bondage of that sin. Many people are leaving the church because of this dogma. Some are leaving the faith altogether.

Additionally, when the B.S. Gospel mentions the Spirit, it usually teaches that His purpose is to convict us of sin so we will work to become more righteous or holy. That message misses the opportunity to talk about our new spiritual self and our daily fellowship with the Spirit. It fails to highlight the greatness of the good news of Jesus and neglects the fact that we can now choose love, which brings life into any situation. And most of all, it abandons God's beautiful, amazing, radical grace.

The Gospel is not just good news; it is great news! It should drive us to our feet as we lift our hands up to the sky, smile big, and say, *"Hallelujah!"*

For additional information on the Bootstrap Gospel, read *Chapter 21, The Bootstrap Gospel,* in *Radical Grace.*

Congratulations! You have completed the foundation of radical grace!

In the next chapter, I offer practical ways to apply what you have learned to things you hear and read. In the final chapter, I offer you some encouragement for living and walking in radical grace.

Chapter 11

Keys

"Be diligent to present yourself approved to God, a worker who does not need to be ashamed, rightly dividing the word of truth."

2 Timothy 2:15

In this chapter, I present the keys that help unlock the truth of a scripture or other teaching. I covered this topic well in my book *Radical Grace*, so I am taking a different approach here. For this lesson, I will first briefly describe each key that is created using what you learned from the last ten chapters. Then, I give you an exercise that you can do to practice rightly dividing the Word by applying the keys. This exercise will help you be confident in any scripture interpretation and decide whether you accept or reject a given teaching. You will be able to avoid legalistic-leaning teaching and being led astray from the freedom that you have found in God's radical grace.

Read chapter 22 of *Radical Grace* if you are reading along with this study.

The Keys

Key 1 – Context

One of the most common ways scriptures are misused is by taking them out of context, usually to promote a specific doctrine. Secondary to that issue is that context helps us to understand certain passages. If you are reading a difficult verse, often zooming out a bit helps clarify the verse. You may need to read the whole paragraph, chapter, or even the whole book to get the context of what the author is saying. Additionally, when considering the context of any section of the Word, it is essential to understand when it was written, the current covenant of God the writer was living in or writing about, i.e., before Christ's resurrection or after, who the writer is and what his purpose was for writing, who the readers of the book are, and their culture at the time of the writing. Context is a key that we must be vigilant to consider when we are presented with any form of doctrine, no matter who or where it comes from.

Key 2 – Covenants

Understanding the timing and definitions of the Covenants of God is helpful when interpreting the Bible. The Old and New Covenants are specific to certain dispensations. In other words, when Jesus died, He fulfilled and ended the Old Covenant, and when He resurrected, He began the New Covenant. There was a brief time that He was here on earth fulfilling His ministry, speaking, and teaching which was before the New Covenant began because He hadn't yet died and risen again. Don't overlook this detail.

The New Covenant is very different from the Old Covenant. As believers in Christ and members of the New Covenant, we have many blessings. We are no longer under the Law, we have the Holy Spirit living in us, and we have been made righteous by having received the righteousness of Christ. As New Covenant believers, our new mission is to love God and love others. When considering scriptural doctrine, these divisions of time and distinctions are important. We must consider the covenant context of anything we are studying or hearing.

Key 3 – Law/C.O.D.E.

Grace proclaims that we are no longer under the Law of Moses or required to work for our righteousness. The entire purpose of Jesus' sacrifice was to bring us into right standing with God for our salvation. This means we receive His righteousness not through our own works, but simply by placing our faith in His righteousness.

When any teaching or interpretation of Scripture states that we are to be obedient to works of the Law, the C.O.D.E., or any man-made rule or regulation, as we learned in this study, it is a false gospel. Being able to recognize this legalistic gospel will help you to reject it and remain in the freedom of the true Gospel of Radical Grace.

Key 4 – Dual Nature

Understanding that we have been born again and made new in our spirit is one of the most beneficial keys. Now, we can distinguish our flesh from our spirit in our minds because we know they are separate. This key unlocks our freedom from legalism. We recognize that our flesh is sinful, but we also know that our new identity is our new self, which submits to God's Spirit. Our two natures are against each other. Grasping duality frees us from the preoccupation of sin and works and leads us into a life lived in love, the Spirit, and the freedom God gave us through His grace. Trust in grace so much that you concentrate not on your sinful flesh but instead on your spiritual purpose.

Key 5 – Sanctification/Righteousness

This key goes hand in hand with duality. We are already made holy and righteous by Jesus, so any doctrine, teaching, song lyric, book, or article that says otherwise is false. Many teachings assume that we need to work on becoming more holy. These teachings emphasize our sins and the need to do better. This focus is a waste of time and energy since, as believers, Jesus already conquered our sins and gave us His righteousness. Instead, our emphasis should be walking in that new holiness and righteousness. The cup isn't half empty; it is full and overflowing! As we learn to walk in the Spirit, our outer actions will better align with our newly transformed inner self. Teachings that ignore the truth of our sanctification and justification are misleading and dangerous.

Key 6 – Spirit

The Spirit is misunderstood by many in the Christian community. Teaching on the Spirit is often neglected or focused only on one of His ministries, not all of them. This key ensures that we keep the Spirit in mind and understand that His ministry toward us is a 24/7 endeavor. He is available to us as He lives in us. He not only baptizes us into the family of God, but He is here to help and guide us every moment. If we ignore that He is in us to help us, we can easily drift into thinking we can do things on our own (like making ourselves holy), which leads to dead works and drives us away from grace.

Key 7 – Jesus/Grace

In this study, we have discussed the Jesus + doctrines and doctrines void of grace. It is incredible how prevalent these doctrines are. Usually, the lack of grace is very subtle, so we don't always catch it. We know the enemy is sneaky, and he will subtly attempt to lead us away from the very God who saved us. This key seems obvious, but you would be surprised how often teachers leave Jesus out of their teachings. Grace is also often left out. Many teachings rely on our works and behavior instead of what Jesus did for us. Anything that counters the Gospel of Grace because it is works-based instead of what Jesus has done is false. Be mindful of anything that doesn't mention Jesus or His grace.

Practice the Keys

In this section, I present an example of how the keys can help you stay in the truth of the Word. This example is a scripture that is often misinterpreted but can be easily interpreted using the keys I have given you.

We will begin by looking at the following verse from Galatians chapter five.

"Stand fast therefore in the liberty by which Christ has made us free, and do not be entangled again with a yoke of bondage."

Galatians 5:1 NKJV

Oftentimes the *"do not be entangled again with a yoke of bondage"* spoken by Paul here is interpreted as *"don't ever sin."* Is the **yoke of bondage** speaking about sin? Or could it be something else? Use the keys to unlock the truth. I ask you questions to help guide you through the process.

Paul used the word, *therefore*. When someone uses the word *therefore*, we should look at what it is *there for*; look at what he previously said. Read chapter four to look at the context of what Paul was saying.

What was Paul talking about in the previous chapter?

What does Paul say the bondwoman and the freewoman symbolize in verse 24?

Paul states in verse 31 that we are children of whom?

What is the key point that Paul is making in chapter four?

What are the next verses, **Galatians 5:2-6**, speaking about?

What covenant were the people of Galatia a part of at the time of this writing?

What are the New Covenant believers freed from? Why?

If Paul is talking about believers having liberty and being freed from the Law, in that context, what might he be warning us against when he said *"do not be entangled again?"*

How does the ***Jesus/Grace*** key help to unlock truth about this verse?

After carefully examining Galatians 5:1, we see that the yoke of bondage is the Law, not sin. Paul didn't tell the Galatians and us never to sin again; he said not to get caught up in trying to fulfill the Law because we are no longer under the Law but under grace. We can stand fast in liberty!

Use the Keys

Now that you know and understand the bricks that form the foundation of radical grace, I encourage you to re-do studies that you have done in the past and re-read the Bible with grace in mind. Consider grace and the keys when you hear or read sermons, songs, and social media posts. You will see whether they are true or not and be able to avoid false doctrine.

Trust the Spirit

One of the many blessings of being a follower of Christ is that He sent the Holy Spirit to live in us. He is the same Spirit who lived in the writers of the New Testament. When you read the Bible, you can trust that the Spirit will reveal things to you. Many people pray before they approach their reading and ask the Spirit to teach them, guide them, and give them wisdom concerning what they are reading. Asking the Spirit for help is good practice because He is God living in us; He is the perfect one to help us know truth from falsehood. We need to trust the Spirit to direct us and help us to understand the Word.

Use your discernment and know that you have a direct relationship with the one who is called the Word. You do not need others, including those who declare they know more than you, to interpret and understand the Bible. No one is between you and your God. Don't just take whatever anyone says as *"gospel truth"* until you have checked it out. Think logically, critically, and trust the Spirit to help you.

Chapter 12

Radical Grace & Fortified Faith

"The grace of our Lord Jesus Christ be with you all. Amen."

Revelation 22:21

You have cemented 24 bricks into your foundational understanding of God's radical grace. You have committed to receiving the biblical perspective on everything from Jesus as the cornerstone to walking according to the Spirit in love. Each brick you have dedicated to your fundamental interpretation of the Gospel bolsters your faith and relationship with your Lord, Jesus. Your new understanding of the depths of radical grace is a springboard for you to leap off into the living water of a life free from shame, doubt, and fear and to walk in steadfast faith.

Starting with a knowledge of a concept is essential. Still, until you put that knowledge into action, it is like memorizing a delicious cookie recipe yet never baking it to enjoy the sweet and satisfying creation it could be. It is time to enjoy the benefits of what grace can do for you as you walk in faith. I encourage you to apply what you have learned to your life. Practice walking in love and grace and experience the beauty of what God will do.

In today's lesson, I offer you practical examples of how you can apply God's radical grace to your own life and begin to see the astonishing value of doing so.

Read chapters 23-26 of *Radical Grace* if you are reading along with this study.

Radical Grace and Faith in Action

Grace for Yourself

God's radical grace frees you from condemnation, tireless work of trying to be perfect, and shame for not measuring up. As I have said before, life is messy. While you are forgiven, you sin, and while you hope to walk in love, sometimes you don't. This uneasy relationship between your flesh and spirit will not go away until you shed your flesh on your trip through the clouds to eternity. You must have grace with yourself first to have grace with others. If Jesus can bestow His grace on you, you can receive it not just for past sins but for present and future ones as well. Take advantage of your newly fortified faith and trust that Jesus died so that you can do just that.

When you realize that you have done something to hurt someone, first, don't beat yourself up over it. Recognize your mistake, but also recognize that you have limits on what you can handle each moment. However, if you stop there in this process, you use grace as an excuse instead of a catalyst for reconciliation and healing. Grace allows you not to wallow in your mistakes, but it is also the motivator to make things better.

Radical grace can resolve conflict and build lasting, loving relationships. Next, we will discuss walking in grace during times of conflict, and then we will look at how grace can bless marriages, families, and friendships.

Grace in Conflict

When you are engaged in conflict with others, that is the exact time you must trust that God's grace is the answer. God's radical grace covers those situations and can bring peace as you submit to the Spirit and seek to obey Jesus' command to love.

The goal of walking by faith, in the Spirit, and living in grace is to love. That means God calls you to wrap the situation in love when you argue with a loved one, feel betrayed by a friend, or are angered by a co-worker. How do you do that? The following questions encourage you to think about how you will seek God and His grace during difficult situations. These things are not easy to do when you are in your defiant flesh, but they are possible when you set your old self aside and seek to put the Spirit in the middle of every situation.

Read *Philippians 2:3*. How would you apply this concept of esteeming others better than yourself to your next argument with someone?

Explain how your strong faith will help you to lay aside selfish ambition in the future.

Read *2 Corinthians 5:16*. If you do *not* look at someone in the flesh, what is it, specifically, that you are not looking at?

How will this act of grace help you now, and in the future, resolve conflict with others?

Read *1 Peter 3:8-9*. Developing compassion for others is an important step in resolving conflict. In what ways does having compassion for others speak to God's grace?

How can you apply radical grace to your future arguments so you may bless instead of revile others?

Read **Romans 12:16**. How does your faith influence your humility?

It is always a good idea to take some time for self-reflection when you conflict with others. This reflection exercise will help you to not *"be wise in your own opinion"* and to put yourself in someone else's shoes. Describe how this process allows you to use God's example of grace to guide you into walking in grace.

Read **Romans 12:18**. This verse admits that sometimes, no matter how much we strive to live in peace with others, because they have a choice, peace might not be achieved if they are unwilling to seek it. What can you still do in those situations that are gracious and loving?

How can your belief in radical grace impact how you live peaceably with others?

Read **_Colossians 3:12-13_**. Faith plays a profound role in the process of forgiveness. Explain how.

Whether the conflict is resolved or not, how can forgiving others affect your life?

Is there someone in your life right now that you need to forgive? How can you apply what you have learned in this study to begin that process?

Read **_Colossians 3:14-15_** and **_Romans 12:9_**. What do you think Paul meant by saying love is the bond of perfection?

What does it mean to not love hypocritically?

Love can transform a difficult situation. In what ways can you change the way you approach conflict in the future to promote love and grace? Explain.

Grace in Relationships

When you walk in faith and apply God's radical grace to your relationships, during times of conflict or not, you will see beautiful blessings bloom from that living water. Examine the following questions and provide your thoughts. Even if your current situation doesn't exactly match the examples I give, contemplate the answers anyway, as they will help you with any relationship you may have.

How can steadfast faith and radical grace help strengthen your marriage today?

Considering what you have learned in this study about grace and love, how can that knowledge be used to produce love and peace in your relationships with your children?

What are some specific things you can teach your children about grace that will help them to get along better with others?

How can sharing your faith and applying grace to your relationships with those who struggle with sin, depression, or self-doubt help their healing process?

Who has given you grace, and how did that affect you?

Thank you for spending time with me during this study. I pray this study has blessed you and helped you acquire unshakeable knowledge of the Gospel of Radical Grace. I also hope that through the process, you have obtained an immoveable faith and deeper relationship with your Lord, Jesus.

May the love and peace of God permeate your heart and mind and the Gospel of Radical Grace fill you with hope and joy.

Love, Laurel

Acknowledgements

I thank You, my Lord and my God, for giving me everything that I needed to complete this project: Yourself, life, an ability to read, Your Word, perseverance, the person who invented the delete and backspace buttons, Your grace, love, and presence. Also, for the encouragement to keep at it on the hard days. Thank you for loving me and showing me that I have value. Thank you for your radical grace.

Phillip, my beloved, again, you have been my biggest cheerleader. Thank you for teaching me so much about grace and sharing your wisdom and time with me as we worked out all the kinks in this study guide together. I cannot describe how your thoughts, prayers, and encouragements have blessed me and this project. Thank you for your dedication to Jesus and the Gospel of Radical Grace. Thank you for making me laugh, for hugging me tight, and for making my coffee.

Thank you, my sweet kids and grandkids. You are all a beautiful picture of what God's radical grace can do for a family. Thank you for being who you are and showing the world what walking by faith and living by grace looks like. You will truly never know what joy you bring to me and how much I love you.

I would like to thank you, Deanna Martin. You have faithfully supported me throughout the years, offered much encouragement and many giggles. Thank you for your love and support and for sticking with me along this rollercoaster we call life.

To my beloved brothers and sisters at Matt's House, I want you to know that I am blessed by your fellowship, love, and friendship. You bring me such joy. Thank you for being a part of my life.

About the Author

LAUREL APPEL, award-winning author of *Radical Grace: Live Free and Unashamed,* is a seasoned Bible teacher with over twenty-five years of experience. She is dedicated to freeing individuals into the grace of God through her insightful books and Bible studies. Laurel's relatable message, drawn from a tapestry of life experiences, resonates deeply with her readers and listeners.

Laurel is married to her best friend, co-worker in ministry, and junior-high sweetheart, Phillip. Together they reside in North Carolina where they nurture their love for Jesus and family. They are parents to three remarkable grown children, two of whom have blessed them with their spouses and daughters.

In addition to her writing ministry, Laurel co-leads ministries with Phillip at *Matt's House* both online and at their in-home fellowship. Laurel and Phillip also co-host the podcast *On the Table* with their daughter, Taylor, and her husband, Michael which will be released in late 2024.

When she's not busy with ministry or writing, Laurel enjoys playing with her granddaughters, painting, or playing her clarinet. She finds joy in simple pleasures like savoring coffee on the back deck and watching the butterflies flittering about in her garden.

For more information about Laurel and her books, or to subscribe to her email list, visit her website at www.laurelappel.com.
Don't forget to follow her on Facebook.com/LaurelAppelAuthor and Instagram.com/LaurelAppel.

If you enjoyed either (or both) *Fortify Your Faith* or *Radical Grace*, the best way to show your support is to write a review anywhere and everywhere books are sold, as well as on Goodreads.com. Your support is greatly appreciated!